THE

BIRDS OF CANADA:

WITH DESCRIPTIONS OF THEIR

PLUMAGE, HABITS, FOOD, SONG, NESTS, EGGS,
TIMES OF ARRIVAL AND DEPARTURE.

BY

ALEXANDER MILTON ROSS,

M.D., M.A., M.R.S.L., ENG.

MEMBER OF THE ROYAL LINNÆAN SOCIETY OF BELGIUM ; MEMBER OF THE
ENTOMOLOGICAL SOCIETIES OF ENGLAND, BELGIUM, UNITED STATES,
AND CANADA ; CORRESPONDING MEMBER OF THE ZOOLOGICAL
SOCIETY OF ENGLAND, ETC.

———————

SECOND EDITION.

———————

ILLUSTRATED.

———————

1872.

British Library Cataloguing-in-Publication Data
A catalogue record for this book is available from the
British Library

Ornithology

Ornithology is a branch of zoology that concerns the study of birds. Etymologically, the word 'ornithology' derives from the ancient Greek ὄρνις *ornis* (bird) and λόγος *logos* (rationale or explanation). The science of ornithology has a long history and studies on birds have helped develop several key concepts in evolution, behaviour and ecology such as the definition of species, the process of speciation, instinct, learning, ecological niches and conservation. Whilst early ornithology was principally concerned with descriptions and distributions of species, ornithologists today seek answers to very specific questions, often using birds as models to test hypotheses or predictions based on theories. However, most modern biological theories apply across taxonomic groups, and consequently, the number of professional scientists who identify themselves as 'ornithologists' has declined. That this specific science has become part of the biological mainstream though, is in itself a testament to the field's importance.

Humans observed birds from the earliest times, and Stone Age drawings are among the oldest indications of an interest in birds, primarily due to their importance as a food source. One of the first key texts on ornithology was Aristotle's *Historia Animalium* (350 BC), in which he noted the habit of bird migration, moulting, egg laying and life span. He also propagated several, unfortunately false myths, such as the idea that swallows hibernated in winter. This idea became so well established, that even as late as 1878, Elliott Coues (an American surgeon, historian and ornithologist) could list as many as 182 contemporary publications dealing with the hibernation of swallows. In the Seventeenth century, Francis Willughby (1635–1672) and John Ray (1627–1705) came up with the first major system of bird classification that was based on function and morphology rather than on form or behaviour, this was a major breakthrough in terms of scientific thought, and Willughby's *Ornithologiae libri tres* (1676), completed by John Ray is often thought to mark the beginning of methodical ornithology. It was not until the Victorian era though, with the emergence of the gun and the concept of natural history, that ornithology emerged as a specialized science. This specialization led to the formation in Britain of the British Ornithologists' Union in 1858, and the following year, its journal *The Ibis* was founded.

This sudden spurt in ornithology was also due in part to colonialism. The bird collectors of the Victorian era observed the variations in bird forms and habits across geographic regions, noting local specialization and variation in widespread species. The collections of museums and private collectors grew with contributions from various parts of the world. This spread of the science meant that many amateurs became interested in 'bird watching' – with real possibilities to contribute knowledge. As early as 1916, Julian Huxley wrote a two part article in the *Auk*, noting the tensions between amateurs and professionals and suggesting that the 'vast army of bird-lovers and bird-watchers could begin providing the data scientists needed to address the fundamental problems of biology.' Organizations were started in many countries and these grew rapidly in membership, most notable among them being the Royal Society for the Protection of Birds (RSPB), founded in 1889 in Britain and the Audubon Society, founded in 1885 in the US.

Today, the science of ornithology is thriving, with many practical and economic applications such as the management of birds in food production (grainivorous birds, such as the Red billed Quelea are a major agricultural pest in parts of Africa), and the study of birds, as carriers of human diseases, such as Japanese Encephalitis, West Nile Virus, and H5N1. Of course, many species of birds have been driven to (or near) extinction by human activities, and hence ornithology has played an important part in conservation, utilising many location specific approaches. Critically endangered species such as the California Condor have been captured and bred in captivity, and it is hoped that many more birds can be saved in a like manner.

PREFACE

TO THE FIRST EDITION.

My object in presenting this volume to the public is in some measure to supply a want long felt by those interested in the study of Canadian Ornithology.

This work is simply, as the title page states, a description of the plumage, habits, food, song, nests, eggs, times of arrival and departure of the birds of Canada.

The birds described consist of the permanent and summer residents, and also such birds as regularly or accidentally stop in Canada during the spring and autumn migrations.

I have in my collection a specimen of each bird described, except a few of the sea birds that frequent the coasts of New Brunswick and Nova Scotia.

The information given as to the food and habits of our birds may probably interest and benefit the agriculturist. The great majority of our feathered visitors are insectivorous, and consequently good friends of the farmer, who should extend his protecting care to these little insect-destroyers.

Many of our Canadian birds are extremely interesting ; and, in beauty of plumage and sweetness and variety of song, equal, if they do not surpass, the birds of any other country.

The arrangement and classification, and the names that are given in this work, are those which have been sanctioned by modern ornithologists.

Toronto, *December*, 1871.

PREFACE

TO THE SECOND EDITION.

———

THE First Edition of this work having been exhausted within a few weeks of its appearance, I have carefully revised this—the second.

Appended is a Classified Catalogue of the Birds of Manitoba and British Columbia, Provinces which now form a portion of the Dominion of Canada.

A Synopsis of the Birds of Canada, with Common and Technical Names, will be found at the end of the work.

I am much indebted to those of my scientific and literary friends who have reviewed this work favorably or otherwise, especially to the latter, for many valuable suggestions.

With the hope that this edition will meet with the same generous approval and patronage as the first, I place it in the hands of my Publishers.

A. M. R.

EVERGREEN GROVE,
Toronto, *July*, 1872.

CONTENTS.

INTRODUCTION.

THE Birds of Canada may be divided into two classes — *Granivorous* and *Carnivorous*. Some of our birds, however, hold a middle nature, and partake of both. They may also be divided into six Orders—The Order of *Raptores*, or Birds of Prey ; the Order of *Scansores*, or Climbers ; the Order of *Insessores*, or Perchers ; the Order of *Rasores*, or Scratchers ; the Order of *Grallatores*, or Waders ; the Order of *Natatores*, or Swimmers ; and again subdivided into Sub-Orders, Families, and Sub-Families.

ORDER I.—RAPTORES *or* BIRDS OF PREY.

Are mostly birds of large size, having strong hooked bills, sharp claws, great extent of wing, and powerful muscles ; the females are generally larger than the males. Birds of this Order live in pairs, such as Eagles, Hawks, Buzzards, and Owls.

· FAMILY FALCONIDÆ. — *The Falcons.* — The birds of this Family are characterized by a robust and strong form ; short bill, curved downward ; round nostrils ; wings long, pointed, adapted for rapid flight. The claws are strong, large, and very sharp. Plumage, generally mottled-grey, black, brown, and white.

FAMILY STRIGIDÆ.—*The Owls.*—The Owls have a large head, short and heavy form, and some have tufts of feathers that somewhat resembles the ears of quadrupeds. Their flight is slow, but strong, and without noise ; their eyes very large ; bill, powerful and curved ; legs, feathered to the toes. Plumage, soft and mottled.

ORDER II.—SCANSORES *or* CLIMBERS.

Birds of this Order have their toes in pairs—two in front and two behind—which especially facilitate climbing. The *Cuculidæ*, or Cuckoo Family, and the *Picidæ*, or Woodpecker Family, belong to this Order.

FAMILY CUCULIDÆ. — *The Cuckoos.* — The Cuckoos are characterized by a long clinical and slender bill ; tail, has ten feathers of graduated length ; wings, long ; plumage, olive-green above, white beneath ; toes, two in front, and two behind.

FAMILY PICIDÆ. — *The Woodpeckers.* — The Woodpeckers have a strong, straight bill; tongue, long ; tail feathers, pointed and shafted ; toes, two in front, and two behind ; wings, short and rounded.

ORDER III.—INSESSORES *or* PERCHERS.

This Order embraces a greater number of species than any other, and comprehends all those birds which live habitually among trees, with the exception of birds of prey and climbing birds. All true perching birds have three toes before, and one behind.

FAMILY HIRUNDINIDÆ. — *The Swallows.* — The Swallows have a short, triangular bill ; large mouth ; wings, long ; tail, more or less forked ; legs, short and delicate ; toes, three in front, and one behind ; plumage, bright metallic blue above, white or reddish beneath.

FAMILY CAPRIMULGIDÆ.—*The Goatsuckers.*— The three members of this Family that visit

Canada, are characterized by a very short triangular bill; gape, large; the inner toe with three joints, the others with four; plumage, soft, lax, and mottled like the Owls.

FAMILY COLOPTERIDÆ.— *The Flycatchers.*— The birds of this Family are noted for their activity and courage. The bill is sharp, strong, broad, and slightly bent down and notched. Wings and tail, about the same length. Three toes in front, and one behind. Plumage, shaded black and gray.

FAMILY TURDIDÆ. — *The Thrushes.* — The Thrushes have the wings and tail rounded, and rather short, with one exception, that of the Brown Thrush, which has a very long tail. The plumage is brown above, and white-spotted with black and brown beneath.

FAMILY SYLVICOLIDÆ.—*The Warblers.*—The birds of this Family are quite numerous, small in size, with sharp and short bills; plumage, variable; legs, long and slender, hind toe shorter than the middle one; claws, curved and sharp.

FAMILY FRINGILLIDÆ.—*The Finches.*—All the birds of this Family are characterized by short and stout bills; wings, long and pointed; legs, black and slender; toes, three before and one behind; plumage, very variable.

ORDER IV.—RASORES *or* SCRATCHERS.

Comprises birds which live mainly upon the ground, and feed principally upon berries, buds, tender leaves, and grain; such as Doves, Grouse, Partridges, and Turkeys.

FAMILY TETRAONIDÆ.—*The Grouse.*—The legs are densely feathered; toes, naked; tail, has sixteen feathers, sometimes eighteen; plumage, black, brown, and mottled.

ORDER V.—GRALLATORES *or* WADERS.

Birds of this Order live near the water, and comprise the Herons, Cranes, Bitterns, Plovers, Snipes, Phalaropes, Sandpipers, and Rails.

FAMILY ARDEIDÆ.—*The Herons.*—The birds of this Family have very long and strong bills; legs, very long and slender, middle toe connected with the outer by a basal web; head, crested; throat, tufted with long feathers.

FAMILY STERINÆ.—*The Terns.*—The Terns have slender, straight, and long bills, curved and pointed ; tail, forked ; feet, webbed ; wings, very long and pointed.

FAMILY COLYMBIDÆ. — *The Divers.* — Have long, pointed, and compressed bills; toes, long and webbed ; legs, situated far behind ; tail, short; wings, short.

The Sub-Family *Podicipinæ*, the Grebes, have short wings ; sides of the head, tufted ; plumage, soft ; bill, long and compressed ; tail, a mere tuft of soft feathers.

FAMILY ALCIDÆ.—Sub-Family *Alcinæ.*—*The Auks.*—The Auks are characterized by a short, broad, and strong body ; wings, short ; tail, short ; bill, about as long as the head, and hooked at the base ; legs and feet, stout and strong ; toes, webbed.

Many species of birds that were quite common in Canada at the beginning of this century, are now rarely seen, and several have become extinct in comparatively recent times.

BIRDS OF CANADA

ORDER I.—Raptores. (Birds of Prey.)

FAMILY FALCONIDÆ.

Sub-Family FALCONINÆ.—*The Falcons.*

PEREGRINE FALCON, OR DUCK HAWK.

Falco anatum.—The Peregrine Falcon.

This bold and spirited falcon arrives in Canada about the last of March, and remains until late in the fall. Color, above, bluish cinereous, with transverse bands of brownish-black ; underneath, yellowish-white, with spots of black on the breast and abdomen ; bill, light blue ; legs and toes, yellow. Length, twenty inches. Its food consists principally of ducks and other water-fowl. Nests, on a high rocky cliff; eggs, four, of a reddish-brown color, covered with dark blotches.

SPARROW HAWK.

Tinnunculus sparverius.—The Sparrow Hawk.

The Sparrow Hawk is a summer resident of Canada. Color, above, light rufous or cinnamon; underneath, pale rufous, spotted with black; quills, brownish-black, with white bars; legs, yellow; bill, light blue. Nests, in a hollow tree; eggs, four, of a yellowish-buff color, covered with spots of reddish-brown. Feeds upon small birds, mice, and squirrels.

Falco columbarius.—The Pigeon Hawk.

This bird arrives in Canada about the middle of March. Length, fourteen inches. Color, above, bluish-slate; forehead and throat, white;

under-parts, pale yellowish-white, every feather
with a line of brownish-black ; legs, yellow ;
quills, black ; bill, blue. Nests, in low fir-trees ;
eggs, three ; dull yellowish-brown, with reddish-
brown spots. Feeds upon sparrows, robins, and
other small birds.

Sub-Family ACCIPITRINÆ.—*The Hawks.*

Astur atricapillus.—The Goshawk.

This hawk is frequently a resident of Canada
throughout the year. Length, twenty inches.
Color, above, dark ashy-blue; underneath, white,
mottled with ashy-brown ; feet, yellow ; bill,
black ; iris, reddish-orange. Builds its nest
upon the branches of a large tree, near the
trunk ; eggs, three or four in number, of a dull
bluish-white, slightly spotted with reddish-brown.
Feeds upon ducks and other water-fowl, as well
as pigeons, blackbirds, and squirrels.

Accipiter Cooperii.—Cooper's Hawk.

This pretty hawk is fifteen inches in length.
Color, above, dark ashy-brown ; underneath,
transversely barred with light rufous and white.
This bird is the smallest of the so-called " Hen
Hawks." It feeds upon poultry and small birds.
Usually builds its nest in the tops of tall pines ;
eggs, four in number, of a bluish-white, with
light brown spots. This hawk is a summer
resident of Canada.

Accipiter fuscus.—The Sharp-shinned Hawk.

The Sharp-shinned Hawk is twelve inches in length. Color, above, brownish-black; underneath, light rufous, with transverse bands of white. Legs, slender; tail, ashy-brown, tipped with white. Feeds upon sparrows and other small birds. This is one of the earliest arrivals of spring, and remains until the last of November. Nests, in a tree; eggs, four, bluish-white.

Sub-Family BUTEONINÆ.—*The Buzzard Hawks.*

Buteo borealis.—The Red-tailed Hawk.

This fine hawk is a resident of Canada throughout the year. Length, twenty-four inches. Color, above, dark umber brown; underneath, pale yellowish-white, with lines and spots of reddish-brown; tail, bright rufous, tipped with white. Feeds upon domestic fowls, partridges, and rabbits. Nests, in a large tree; eggs, three in number, of a yellowish-white, with dark blotches.

Buteo lineatus.—The Red-shouldered Hawk.

The Red-shouldered Hawk is eighteen or nineteen inches in length. Color, above, brown; underneath, orange-red; tail, brownish-black; feet, yellow. Nests, in a tree; eggs, five, pale blue, with dark reddish spots. This hawk remains in Canada throughout the year. Feeds upon squirrels, poultry, and small birds.

B. *pennsylvanicus.*—The Broad-winged Hawk.

The Broad-winged Hawk is eighteen inches in length. Color, above, umber-brown ; underneath, white, with reddish spots ; tail, dark brown. This bird is a common resident of Canada during the summer. Nests, in the top of a tall tree ; eggs, four or five, of a yellowish-white color, with light brown spots. Its food consists of small birds, reptiles, and squirrels.

Archibuteo lagopus.—The Rough-legged Hawk.

This bird is twenty inches in length. Color, light brown, mottled with reddish-brown and white. Frequently remains in Canada throughout the year. Nests, in a tall tree ; eggs, four or five, of a bluish-white color, blotched with brown.

A. *sancti johannis.*—The Black Hawk.

The specimen in my collection measures twenty-four inches in length. Color, glossy black, with a brownish tinge about the head and neck. Tail, black, with bands of white. Frequents marshes and swamps. Nests, in the top of a large tree ; eggs, five, of a dirty white color. Remains in Canada throughout the year.

Sub-Family MILVINÆ.—*The Kites.*

Circus hudsonius.—The Marsh Hawk.

The Marsh Hawk is one of our most common summer hawks. It arrives here from the south about the first of May. Color, bluish-cinereous above ; beneath, reddish-white. Nests, on the ground ; eggs, four or five, of a dirty white color. Feeds upon field mice, principally, and the number of these destructive little animals which it devours during the breeding season is almost incredible. It is consequently entitled to the protection of the farmer.

Sub-Family AQUILINÆ.—*The Eagles.*

WHITE-HEADED EAGLE.

Haliætus leucocephalus.—The White-headed
Eagle.

This noble bird is frequently met with on the
high shore of Lake Ontario throughout the year,

and is often seen in the Ottawa region, near the interior lakes, and in the vicinity of the Rideau canal. Feeds upon wild fowl and small animals, and is equally partial to fish. The nest of this species, formed of large sticks, sods, moss, and hay, is usually found in a lofty tree, in a swamp or morass, and, as it is increased or repaired every season, becomes of great size; eggs, two or three, of a yellowish-white color, with brown patches. General color, brownish-black; head and tail, white; bill, feet, and iris, yellow.

Aquila canadensis.—The Golden Eagle.

This magnificent eagle is rarely met with except in the interior of Canada. The general color of the plumage is deep brown, mixed with tawny on the head and neck, the feathers on the back being finely shaded with a darker hue. Feeds upon young fawns, raccoons, rabbits, and large birds. Usually nests on the sides of steep rocky crags; eggs, three in number, of a dull white, with patches of bronze.

Pandion carolinensis.—The Fish-Hawk.

This common and well known hawk is a summer resident of Canada. Color, above, umber-brown; beneath, white; bill and claws, bluish-black. Nests, in a large tree, on the margin of the lakes or rivers; eggs, three in number, of a reddish-cream color. Feeds entirely upon fish.

FAMILY STRIGIDÆ. *THE OWLS.*

Sub-Family BUBONINÆ.—*The Horned Owls.*

GREAT HORNED OWL.

Bubo virginianus.—The Great Horned Owl.

The Great Horned Owl is a permanent resident of Canada. It is very destructive to domestic fowls, and consequently very obnoxious to the

2

farmer. Length, twenty-two inches. Color, brownish-black, mottled with ashy-white. The nest of this owl is frequently built in the topmost branches of tall pines, and sometimes in the top of a stub; eggs, three or four, of a yellowish-white.

Scops asio.—Mottled Owl, or Screech Owl.

This owl feeds upon mice and squirrels, small birds, and beetles. Length, ten inches. Color, pale ashy-brown. Breeds in Canada, Nests, in a hollow tree; eggs, four or five, white.

Otus Wilsonianus,—The Long-eared Owl.

The Long-eared Owl feeds upon small birds. It rears its young in nests which it finds, seldom making one for itself; eggs, four or five, of a dirty white color. This owl lingers about mountain streams. Its cry is prolonged and plaintive. Breeds in Canada. Length, fifteen inches. Color, brownish-black, mottled with ashy-white.

Brachyotus Cassinii.—The Short-eared Owl.

This Owl is a permanent resident of Canada. Length, fourteen inches. Color, light brown, mottled with gray. Builds its nest upon the ground; eggs, four in number, pure white. Feeds upon mice and small birds,

Sub-Family SYRNINÆ.—*The Gray Owls.*

Syrnium nebulosum.—The Barred Owl.

This is one of our most common owls. Length, twenty inches. Color, light ashy-brown. Feeds upon small birds, mice, and reptiles. Nests, in high trees; eggs, three in number, white. Remains in Canada throughout the year.

Syrnium cinereum.—The Cinereous Owl.

This is the largest member of the owl family. Length, thirty inches. Color, ashy-brown, mottled with ashy-white. Head, large; eyes small. Feeds upon rabbits, squirrels, and other small animals. It is a rare visitor to this part of Canada. This owl breeds in the far north.

Nyctale Richardsonii.—The Sparrow Owl.

This pretty little owl is a regular winter visitor. It is eleven inches in length; the color, above, white; legs and bill, light yellow. Breeds in the north-west. Nests, in a tree; eggs, four in number, pure white. Its food consists of mice and small birds. Seeks its prey by night.

Nyctale acadica.—The Saw-whet Owl.

This species is a permanent resident of Canada. It is the smallest of the family, being only eight and a-half inches in length. Color, above, reddish-brown ; beneath, ashy-white, with spots of rufous. It builds its nest in a stump or hollow tree ; eggs, four in number, pure white. The food of this owl consists of bats, mice, and small birds.

Sub-Family NYCTEININÆ.— *The Day Owls.*

Surnia ululu.—The Hawk Owl.

The Hawk Owl is a permanent resident of Canada. It possesses many of the characteristics of a falcon. Length, eighteen inches ; the color, pale ashy-brown ; throat, white ; a large brown spot on each side of the breast. This bird seeks its prey by day as well as by night. Nests, in a tree ; eggs, two in number, pure white.

SNOWY OWL.

Nyctea nivea.—The Snowy Owl.

This beautiful owl is a regular fall and winter visitor in Canada. It is twenty-seven inches in length ; the plumage is pure white, with a few spots of dark brown on the back and wings. Its food consists principally of rabbits, birds, and fish, which it obtains by daylight as well as by twilight. The Snowy Owl flies with great rapidity, often capturing ducks and other water fowl upon the wing, Breeds in the arctic regions.

ORDER II.—𝔖cansores. (Climbers.)

FAMILY CUCULIDÆ. *THE CUCKOOS.*

Coccygus americanus.—The Yellow-billed Cuckoo.

The Yellow-billed Cuckoo is a rare visitor in Canada. It is eleven inches in length. Color, above, olive-green, tinged with ash near the bill; beneath, white; tail, olive-green, with a border of black tipped with white; upper mandible, black; lower, yellow; quills, orange-cinnamon. This bird breeds in the United States. Its nest is built in a low tree or shrub; eggs, four, of a bright green color. The song of this cuckoo is discordant and harsh, and may be represented by *kow-kow, kow-kow.* Its food consists of insects and the eggs and young of other birds.

Coccygus erythrophthalmus.—The Black-billed Cuckoo.

This species is a regular summer visitor. It arrives about the tenth of May, and remains until the first of September. In size, color, and characteristics, it closely resembles the preceding bird. It differs only in having both mandibles black. This cuckoo breeds in Canada. Nests in a barberry bush or low tree; eggs, four, of a bright green color.

FAMILY PICIDÆ. *THE WOODPECKERS.*

Sub-Family PICINÆ.

Picus villosus.—The Hairy Woodpecker.

The Hairy Woodpecker is a permanent resident of Canada. Its food consists principally of insects and their larvæ. Color, black and white, spotted. Length, eleven inches. Nests, in a hole in a tree ; eggs, five, pure white.

Picus pubescens.—The Downy Woodpecker.

This woodpecker is six inches in length. Color, above, black, with a white band down the back ; two white stripes on the side of the head ; the lower parts white. Nests, in a hole in a tree ; eggs, six, pure white. The food of this bird consists entirely of insects and their larvæ.

Picoides articus.—The Black-backed, Three-toed Woodpecker.

This species is a permanent resident of Canada. Its habits do not differ from those of other woodpeckers. Back, black ; wings, spotted white and black ; top of head, saffron color. Nests, in a stump ; eggs, four, pure white.

Sphyrapicus varius.—Yellow-bellied Woodpecker.

This pretty bird is a summer resident of Canada. It is often seen in orchards, especially in apple-trees. Feeds upon insects and their larvæ. Back and wings, spotted black and white ; top of head and throat, red ; belly, yellow. This bird is a friend to the farmer, as it destroys immense numbers of insects. Nests, in a decayed tree in the woods; eggs, five, pure white.

Centurees carolinensis.—The Red-bellied Woodpecker.

The Red-bellied Woodpecker is a common summer resident of Canada. It possesses all the active and noisy habits characteristic of its family. Length, ten inches. Color, above, black, crossed with white ; wings, black, tipped with bars of white ; head, neck, and shoulders, glossy red ; cheeks and under sides of the neck, pale buff ; breast and abdomen, yellowish-ash, stained with bright red ; legs and feet, bluish-green ; iris, red. Nests, in a hollow limb ; eggs, four, pure white. This species seldom appears about orchards or open grounds ; but it often visits corn fields in search of grain, of which it is particularly fond. Its principal food is insects, which it obtains from decayed trees after the manner of other woodpeckers.

Picoides hirsutus.—The Banded Three-toed Woodpecker.

This woodpecker is a permanent resident of Canada. Length, nine inches. Black, above ; white, beneath ; quills, spotted with white ; top of the head, spotted with white ; the crown of the male, with a yellow patch. Nests, in a stump or decayed tree ; eggs, four, creamy-white.

Hylatomus pileatus.—The Pileated Woodpecker.

This beautiful woodpecker is seldom seen in the settled portions of Canada, although it is frequently met with in the interior. It is the largest and most powerful of the woodpecker family. General color of body, wings, and tail, greenish-black ; a narrow white streak just above the eye to the occiput ; crown of head, bright red. Length, eighteen inches. Nests, in a hole in a tree or stub; eggs, five in number, pure white.

RED-HEADED WOODPECKER.

Melanerpes crythrocephalus.—The Red-headed Woodpecker.

This bird is one of our regular visitors. It arrives here from the south about the middle

3

of May. Its habits are the same as those of
the other species, except that he is a great
lover of fruit and grain. It is, however, a
question whether he is not a greater friend
than enemy to the farmer, as he kills great
numbers of insects. Back, black ; belly, white ;
head and neck all round, crimson. Length, ten
inches ; bill and feet, black. Nests, in a hole in
a stub or tree ; eggs, four in number, pure white.

GOLDEN-WINGED WOODPECKER.

Colaptes auratus.—Golden-winged Woodpecker.

The Golden-winged Woodpecker is one of our
best known and most beautiful summer visitors.

It is twelve inches long ; the wing six inches. The top of the head, and the upper part of the neck, bluish-ash ; a red crescent on the nape ; the other upper parts, olive brown, with transverse bands of black ; the lower parts, yellowish white, tinged with a brownish, and ornamented with circular black spots, and with a black crescent on the breast ; the shafts and under surfaces of the wings are gamboge yellow. This elegant bird arrives in Canada from the south about the twentieth of April, and returns late in the fall. Nests, in a hollow tree ; eggs, six, pure white. Feeds upon insects, berries, and grains.

ORDER III.—Insessores. (Perchers.)

FAMILY TROCHILIDÆ. *THE HUMMING BIRDS.*

Trochilus colubris.—The Ruby-throated Humming Bird.

This beautiful little bird arrives here from the south about the last of May. Nests, in a tree ; eggs, two, pure white. Its food consists of insects and the juice of sweet-scented flowers.

FAMILY CYPSELIDÆ. *THE SWIFTS.*

Cheturæ pelasgia.—The Chimney Swallow.

This swallow arrives here about the last of May. Leaves for the south about the first of September. Color, sooty-brown. Nests, in hollow trees or unused chimneys ; eggs, five, pure white. Feeds upon insects.

Family HIRUNDINIDÆ. *THE SWALLOWS.*

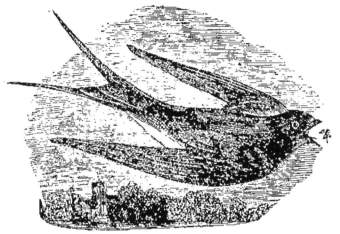

BARN SWALLOW.

Hirundo americana.—The Barn Swallow.

The general color of this swallow is steel-blue above ; beneath, light chestnut ; tail, forked. Receives its name from its frequently attaching its nest to the rafters in barns. Feeds upon insects.

H. lunifrons.—The Cliff Swallow.

The Cliff Swallow is black, above ; white, beneath ; tail, green. Builds its nest under projecting cliffs ; eggs, six, white, with a purplish tint. Feeds upon insects.

H. riparia.—The Bank Swallow.

This is the smallest of the swallows. Color, above, grayish-brown ; beneath, pure white. It takes its name from its habit of making deep, winding holes in sand banks, in which it builds its nest ; eggs, four, pure white. Feeds upon insects.

H. bicolor.—The White-breasted Swallow.

This well-known swallow arrives here about the middle of May. Color, above, metallic-green ; beneath, white. Nests, in a hole in a tree or stub, and sometimes in a martin's box ; eggs, four, white. Feeds upon insects.

Progne purpurea.—The Purple Martin.

This pretty and interesting bird arrives in Canada early in April. Color : the old males are glossy steel-blue all over ; the females are glossy steel-blue above, and pale brown beneath. Two broods are raised during the season. Nests, in a hole in a tree, or martin's box ; eggs, four or six, pure white. Early in September the martins leave for the south.

FAMILY CAPRIMULGIDÆ. *THE GOAT-SUCKERS.*

WHIP-POOR-WILL.

Caprimulgus vociferus.—The Whip-poor-will.

The Whip-poor-will is a regular summer resident of Canada. It is ten and a-half inches long; bill, short, and bent at the point; mouth, very large, and beset along the sides with a number of stiff bristles, which turn inwards; eyes, full and large; the plumage is variegated with black, pale cream-brown, and rust color. The notes of the whip-poor-will are three, and have a resemblance to the syllables "*whip poor will*," from which it takes its name. It begins its song soon after sunset, and continues till late at night; then remains silent till near the dawn, when it resumes, and continues till sunrise. During the day it sits in the most retired, solitary, and deep-shaded parts of the woods, generally on high ground, where it reposes in silence.

When disturbed, it rises within a few feet, and flies slowly through the woods for thirty or forty yards, and generally settles on a low branch, or on the ground. Its sight appears deficient during the day, as it seems to want that vivacity for which it is distinguished in the morning and evening twilight. It does not perch, like other birds, sitting across the branch, but lengthwise ; and its hinder toe is capable of being turned forward as well as backward. It is solitary in its habits, and is generally seen alone. The female begins to lay about the second week in May, selecting for this purpose the most unfrequented part of the wood, often where some brush, old logs, or heaps of leaves had been lying, and always on a dry situation. The eggs, usually two in number, greenish-white, are deposited on the ground, or on the leaves, not the slightest appearance of a nest being visible. Its food consists entirely of night-flying insects.

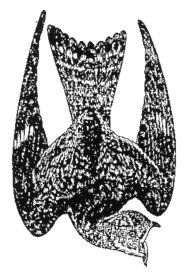

NIGHT HAWK.

Chordeiles popetue.—The Night Hawk.

This is a well known bird. It arrives here from the south about the middle of May. The colors of this bird, though plain, have a beautiful effect from the elegance of their disposition : the plumage being beautifully freckled, barred, and spotted with brown, black, grey, and ferruginous, variously arranged and diversified. The bill is small, flat, and hooked at the tip; the eyes are large, full, and black ; the legs are short, rough, and scaly, and feathered below the knee. The male is distinguished from the female

4

by an oval white spot, near the end of the first three quill feathers. Nests, on the bare ground, sometimes on a rock ; eggs, two, grayish-white, spotted with brown and lavender. Its food consists entirely of moths, gnats, beetles, and other night insects.

C. carolinensis.—The Chuck-will's Widow.

The Chuck-will's Widow closely resembles the Whip-poor-will in general appearance. This interesting bird is a very rare visitor in Canada. It derives its name from its repeated utterance of a cry that exactly resembles the words "*chuck will's widow.*" Like the other members of the Goat Sucker Family, this bird seeks its food by night. Nests, on the ground ; eggs, two, grayish-white, mottled with buff.

SUB-ORDER CLAMATORES.

(SCREAMERS.)

Family ALCEDINIDÆ.   *THE KING-FISHERS.*

BELTED KINGFISHER.

Ceryle alcyon.—The Belted Kingfisher.

This bird is a very common summer resident of Canada. It arrives here about the tenth of April. The plumage of this pretty bird is bright blue above, marked with a great number of dark streaks caused by the blue-black shaft of each feather. The wings are blackish-brown, bound with white, and variegated with blue ; the head, with a crest ; a band across the breast and sides of the same color as the back ; the tail, with transverse bands and spots of white. Length, twelve inches. Nests, in a long winding hole in a sand-bank; eggs, six, pure white. Feeds upon fish,

Family COLOPTERIDÆ. *THE FLY-CATCHERS.*

Sub-Family TYRANNINÆ.—Tyrant Fly-catchers.

KING BIRD.

Tyrannus carolinensis.—The King Bird.

This brave little bird is a summer inhabitant of Canada. Color above, dark bluish-ash, the lower parts white ; the concealed crest, vermillion and orange. Its favorite resorts are open fields or orchards. Feeds upon insects. It is a courageous little bird, and attacks hawks, crows, and other large birds without the least hesitation. Nests, in an orchard tree ; eggs, five, of a beautiful creamy-white color, with spots and specks of brown. Departs for the south, first September.

Myiarchus crinitus.—The Great-crested Fly-catcher.

This bird arrives in Canada about the middle of May. The nest is placed in a hollow tree or stub, and nearly always contains the cast-off skin of a snake, which is coiled at the bottom ; eggs, four, of a dull cream color, scratched with purple lines. Feeds upon insects. The general color of this bird is dull greenish-olive above ; under parts, bright sulphur-yellow ; head, well defined crest. Departs for the south first of September.

Sayornis fuscus.—The Phebe Bird.

This very common bird is too well known to need a description. It arrives from the south about the last of March, and departs the last of October.

Contopus virens.—The Wood Pewee.

This is a common summer resident of Canada. It arrives here about the twentieth of May. General color, dark olive brown ; the lower parts, pale-yellow. This bird loves the dark quiet retreats of the forests. Here, sitting upon a branch, it may be seen watching for insects, uttering its low melancholy notes. Nests, in a tree ; eggs, four or five ; light-yellow, spotted· with red on the large end.

Empidonax minimus.—The least Fly-catcher.

This active little bird arrives from the south about the first of May. Color, above, olive-brown; beneath, yellowish-white; length, five inches. Usually nests in an apple tree; eggs, four; creamy-white color. Feeds upon insects entirely.

SUB-ORDER OSCINES.

(SINGING BIRDS.)

FAMILY TURDIDÆ. *THE THRUSHES.*

WOOD THRUSH.

Turdus mustelinus.—The Wood Thrush.

This sweet songster is a common Canadian visitor, arriving here about the twentieth of May. The Wood Thrush delights in deep, shady places, where there is a small brook. Its soft, half plaintive notes excel in sweetness those of any other Canadian bird. Color, above, clear cinnamon-brown ; the under parts are white, tinged with buff, marked with blackish spots. Nests, in a low shrub in the deep woods ; eggs, four in number, of a blue color, tinted with green. Feeds upon insects.

T. palassii.—The Hermit Thrush.

The Hermit Thrush arrives in Canada about the middle of May. Color, above, olive-brown ; beneath, white ; length, eight inches. Nests, in low trees or bushes ; eggs, four, of a light blue color. In its habits and song it is similar to the Wood Thrush. Feeds upon insects.

T. fuscescens.—The Tawny Thrush.

This is a common summer resident of Canada. Color, above, light reddish-brown ; below, white. Nests, on the ground ; eggs, four, of a bluish-green color. Feeds upon insects.

T. Swainsonii.—The Olive-backed Thrush.

This pretty bird is the least common of all the thrushes. Color, olivaceous ; breast, white ; throat and breast, spotted with brown. Nests, in the deepest recesses of the forest ; eggs, four, of a reddish-brown color. Feeds on insects.

T. migratorious.—The Robin.

This is one of the most common and interesting summer residents.   Color, above, olive-gray ; top and sides of the head, black ; throat, white, streaked with black ; under parts, chestnut-brown ; length, ten inches.   Its food consists of caterpillars, earth-worms, and grubs of various kinds.   Nests, in a tree ; eggs, four, greenish-blue.   The popular prejudice against this bird is unjust.   It is a good friend to the farmer, and should be protected.

Sub-Family MIMINÆ.—*Mocking Birds.*

Harporhynchus rufus.—The Brown Thrush, or Brown Thrasher.

This sweet songster is one of our most welcome visitors.   In the pleasant spring mornings, this bird utters the sweetest melodies from the top-most branches of some isolated tree.   During the day it prefers low thick bushes.   The nest is made in a clump of low bushes, a few feet from the ground ; eggs, four to six, of a dull buff color, sprinkled with brown.   General color, above, light cinnamon-red ; below, pale rufous white. The Brown Thrasher arrives here about the last of April, and departs for its southern home the first week in October.

CAT BIRD.

Galeoscoptes carolinensis.—The Cat Bird.

This well known bird arrives in Canada about the middle of May. Its habits are so well known that a description is hardly necessary. General color, dark plumbeous ; the under tail coverts, dark brown. In spring its song is varied, mellow, and sweet. It possesses to some extent the power to imitate the notes of other birds. Sometimes it mews like a cat, hence its name. Nests, in low bushes ; eggs, four, sometimes six, greenish-blue. It rears two broods in a season. About the middle of October the Cat Bird goes south.

FAMILY SAXICOLIDÆ. *THE ROCK INHABITERS.*

Sialia sialis.—The Blue Bird.

The Blue Bird, is a common summer resident of Canada. General color, above, azure-blue ; beneath, reddish-brown. It is one of the earliest arrivals, making its appearance about the middle

5

of March.   Nests, in a knot-hole or martin's box;
eggs, five in number, of a light-blue color.   Feeds
entirely upon insects.   Leaves for the south the
first of October.

FAMILY SYLVIDÆ. *THE WOOD INHABITERS.*

Regulus calendula.—The Ruby-crowned Wren.

This pretty little wren is at once distinguished
by the crown, which has a concealed patch of
scarlet feathers, which are white at the base.
Its song is charming, and harmonious.   Arrives
here about the middle of May, on its way north
to breed, and visits us again in September, while
migrating south.   Feeds upon insects and their
larvæ.

Regulus satrapa.—The Golden-crested Wren.

This wren is distinguished from the Ruby-
crowned, by a crest of orange-red, encircled by
yellow.   Visits Canada in the spring and autumn.
Breeds north of Ontario.   Feeds upon insects.

Regulus cuvieri.—Cuvier's Golden-crested Wren.

This diminutive and beautiful bird differs from
the Regulus Satrapa in having two black bands
on the crown, separated by a white band.   This
wren usually accompanies the two preceding
species, in their spring and fall migrations.

FAMILY PARIDÆ.

Sub-Family PARINÆ.—*The Titmice.*

Parus atricapillus.—The Black-cap Titmouse, or Chick-a-dee.

This pretty little bird is one of the few species that remain with us throughout the year. It builds its nest in a hole in a stump or tree ; eggs, six in number, white, with reddish-brown markings at the larger end. Two broods are raised in a season. General color, ashy-brown above, and white beneath ; top of the head and throat, black ; and the sides of the head between, white. Feeds entirely upon insects and their larvæ.

P. hudsonicus.—Hudson's Bay Titmouse.

This bird is a permanent resident of Canada. Color, olive brown above ; white beneath ; top of the head, brown ; sides of the head, white. Length, five inches. Nests in a shrub ; eggs, four, pure white.

Sub-Family SITTINÆ.—*The Nuthatches.*

WHITE-BELLIED NUTHATCH.

Sitta carolinensis.—The White-bellied Nuthatch.

This nuthatch is one of our common summer birds, and sometimes remains in Canada through the winter. Color, ashy-blue above; the under parts, white; top of the head and neck, black. Nests, in a hole in a stump or tree; eggs, six, dull white. Feeds upon insects. At night it attaches its feet to the bark of a tree, and sleeps with its head downwards.

S. canadensis.—The Red-bellied Nuthatch. •

The Red-bellied Nuthatch is smaller than the preceding species; the belly, reddish-brown; in other respects it is similar to the White-bellied Nuthatch.

FAMILY CERTHIADÆ. *THE CREEPERS.*

AMERICAN CREEPER.

Certhia americana.—The American Creeper.

This industrious insect-hunter is a permanent resident of Canada. Color, above, dark brown, each feather streaked with white ; the under parts, rusty-brown ; a white streak over the eye. Feeds upon insects and their larvæ. Nests, in a hollow tree ; eggs, six, dark gray.

FAMILY TROGLODYTIDÆ. *THE WRENS.*

Cistothorus palustris.—Long-billed Marsh Wren.

This species lives among the rank vegetation growing in marshes and inlets to the lakes. Here it builds its nest, and lays six eggs of a deep chocolate color. This wren is five and a-half inches long ; the upper parts, dull reddish-brown ; the under parts, and a streak over the eye, white. Feeds upon insects. It arrives here about the middle of May, and leaves for the south about the last of September.

Troglodytes hyemalis.—The Winter Wren.

The Winter Wren arrives in Ontario about the first of October, and remains through the winter, leaving early in the spring for the north, where it breeds. Color, reddish-brown.

Troglodytes œdon.—The House Wren.

This well known and interesting bird arrives from the south the first week in May. It lives entirely upon insects, of which it destroys vast numbers. This little wren delights in living near the habitations of men, and builds its nest in any hole in a tree or stump it finds ; eggs, six, pale reddish-brown. Color, reddish-brown.

Family SYLVICOLIDÆ. *WARBLERS.*

Sub-Family SYLVICOLINÆ.—*The Wood Warblers.*

Mniotilta varia.—The Black and White Creeper.

This is a regular summer resident, Nests, in a low bush ; eggs, four, creamy-white. General color of the male, black ; the feathers broadly edged with white. All the birds of this family are insectivorous. I have thirty species of the warbler family in my collection.

Parula americana.—The Blue Yellow-backed Warbler.

This warbler arrives here about the middle of April, on its way to the north, and returns southward about the middle of September. Color, above, blue, with a yellow stripe on the middle of the back ; beneath, yellowish-white. This species utters a soft, prolonged twitter : its only song.

Geothlypis trichas.—The Maryland Yellow Throat.

This very pretty warbler breeds in Ontario. Color, above, olive-green, tinged with brown ; throat and neck, bright yellow. Nests, in low bushes ; eggs, four, creamy-white.

G. philadelphiæ.—The Mourning Warbler.

Its note is a little chit, uttered in a soft, pensive tone. General color, ash-gray above, and black underneath, Breeds in Canada. Nests, in a low bush ; eggs, four, bluish-white.

G. macgillvraii.—Macgillvray's Warbler.

This Warbler is five inches long, the wing less than two and a-half inches ; the head and neck, ash, a narrow frontlet and space around the eye, black ; the feathers of the forward under parts really black, but appearing gray from the ashy tips of the feathers ; the rest of the upper parts, dark olive-green, and of the lower, yellow. Breeds in Canada. Nests, in a low bush ; eggs, five, flesh-colored.

Dendroica virens—The Black Throated Green Warbler.

The Black-throated Green Warbler is five inches long, the wings over two and a-half inches ; the crown and back, olive ; the forehead, superciliary and maxillary stripes, yellow. Breeds in Canada. Nests, in a bush near the ground ; eggs, five, bluish white.

D. palmarum.—The Yellow Red-poll Warbler.

This bird is five inches long, the wing nearly two and a-half inches, the crown, sides of the head, and inferior streaks, yellow ; a white spot on the end of the tail, superciliary streak and under parts, yellow. Breeds in the interior of Canada. Visits Ontario in May and September.

D. tigrina.—Cape May Warbler.

The Cape May Warbler is five and a-quarter inches long, the wing nearly three inches, the bill, acute and decurved ; the color, olive above, rump and under parts, yellow ; crown, blackish ; sides of the head, chestnut. This pretty bird · breeds in northern Ontario.

D. canadensis.—The Black-Throated Blue Warbler.

This bird is five and a-half inches long, the wing, two and a-half ; the crown, black ; back, ash ; maxillary stripe, white. Breeds in Manitoba. Visits Ontario in the spring and fall.

D. coronata.—The Yellow-rump Warbler.

This Warbler is five and a-quarter inches long, the wing three inches ; the color, slate blue above ; throat, white ; head, blackish ; the sides and rump, with a yellow patch. Breeds north of Ontario.

D. blackburniæ.—Blackburnian Warbler.

This is, without exception, the most beautiful of all the warblers. Color : the back, black ; throat, bright orange ; and a patch on the wing and outer tail feathers, white. Breeds in the far north. Remains for a few days in May and October.

D. castanca.—The Bay-breasted Warbler.

This bird is five inches long; the head, chestnut ; sides of the head, black ; and belly, white. Like most of the family, this bird breeds in the north-

6

ern part of this continent. During the spring and fall migrations it stops for a few days in Ontario.

D. pinus.—The Pine-creeping Warbler.

The Pine-creeping Warbler is five and a-half inches long, and the wing, three inches; olive-green above, and yellow beneath ; two dull white bands upon the wings. Breeds in northern Canada. Nests, on the ground ; eggs, four, bluish-white.

D. pennsylvanica.—The Chestnut-sided Warbler.

This species is five inches long ; the wing, two and a-half inches ; the crown, yellow, encircled with white ; sides of the head, black, enclosing a white patch behind ; and sides of the body, chestnut. Breeds in northern Canada. Visits Ontario in the spring and fall.

D. striata.—The Black-poll Warbler.

This warbler is five and three-quarter inches long; the wing, three inches; the crown and sides, black ; the cheeks below the eye, white. Breeds north of Ontario. Spring and autumn visitor.

D. æstiva.—The Yellow Warbler.

This species arrives here about the middle of May, and breeds here. Nests, in a willow or maple tree ; eggs, four, white, with brown blotches. General color, yellow.

D. maculosa.—The Black and Yellow Warbler.

This bird is a summer resident of Canada. Builds its nest in the willows that grow in low marshy grounds ; eggs, four, pure white.

Myiodioctes canadensis.—The Canada Fly-catcher.

The Canada Fly-catcher is about five and a-third inches long, the wing, about two and two-thirds inches ; the back, bluish ; streaks upon the crown ; stripe on the side of the head and neck ; and breast, black. Breeds in Canada. Nests, on the ground, or in a low bush ; eggs, four, pinkish-white.

M. mitratus.—The Hooded Warbler.

The Hooded Warbler is five inches long ; the head and neck, black ; back, olive-green ; the front, cheeks, and under parts, yellow. It is very rarely seen in Ontario. Breeds in the south. Visits Canada in the spring.

M. minutus.—The Small-headed Fly-catcher.

This little bird is four inches long ; olive, above ; yellow, beneath ; and the wing, with two white bands. Visits Canada in May and October.

M. pusillus.—The Green Black-cap Fly-catcher.

This Fly-catcher is four and three-quarter inches long ; the upper parts, olive ; the forehead,

and under parts, bright yellow ; the crown, with
a black patch.   Remains here for a few days in
May and August.

Helmitherus vermivorus.—The Worm-eating Warbler.

The Worm-eating Warbler is five inches long.
Color, olive-green, above ; beneath, brownish-
yellow.   Visits Canada during the spring and
summer migrations.   Breeds in the far north.

Helminthopaga pinus.—The Blue-winged Yellow Warbler.

This bird is four and a-half inches long ; the
wing, two and four-tenths inches,   Color, above,
olive-green ; the wings and tail, bluish-gray ; the
crown and under parts, rich orange-yellow.   Its
nest is elongated, and attached by its upper edge
to several stout stalks of grass ; eggs, four to six,
pure white, with a few pale red spots at the
larger end.   Breeds in Canada.

H. chrysoptera.—The Golden-winged Warbler.

This beautiful warbler is five inches long;
upper parts bluish-gray ; head and under parts,
black and yellow. Breeds in the interior of
Canada.   Remains in Ontario a few days in the
spring and fall.

H. ruficapilla.—The Nashville Warbler.

The Nashville Warbler is over four and a-half inches long; the wing, two and three-fourths inches; the color, above, olive-green; beneath, dull white; the color, olive-green above; under parts, deep yellow. Visits Canada in the spring and fall.

H. peregrina.—The Tennessee Warbler.

The Tennessee Warbler is four and a-half inches long; the wing, two and three-fourths inches; the color, above, olive-green; beneath, dull white; the top and sides of the head, ashy-gray. Breeds in northern Canada. Spring and fall visitor.

Icteria viridis.—The Yellow-breasted Chat.

This bird is nearly seven inches in length; upper parts, olive-green; under-parts gamboge-yellow. Visits Canada in May and September.

Setophaga ruticilla.—The Red Start.

The Red Start arrives here about the middle of May, and leaves about the fifteenth of September. It is five and a quarter inches long; the wing two and a half inches; the general color, black, the sides of the breast and base of the quills and tail, reddish-orange, and the abdomen, white. This is one of the prettiest and liveliest birds of our forests. The nest is built upon a low bush; eggs, four to six; white, sprinkled with ashy-gray.

Seiurus aurocapillus.—The Golden-crowned Thrush.

This beautiful bird is a summer resident of Canada. It arrives here about the last of April, and departs the last of September. Color, above, olive-green, with a tinge of yellow; crown, with two streaks of black, enclosing a broad orange stripe; beneath, white; the breast and sides of the body, black. It builds its nest on the ground, in the form of an old oven; eggs, five, creamy-white.

S. noveboracensis.—The Water Thrush, or Wagtail.

The Water Thrush arrives here about the first of May; departs twentieth of September. Color, above, olive-brown; beneath, pale sulphur-yellow, brightest on the abdomen. It can be found near brooks, rivers, or ponds, wading in the shallow water in search of aquatic insects, continually wagging its tail. Nests, in a swamp; eggs, five, reddish-brown.

Sub-Family TANAGRINÆ.—*The Tanagers.*

Pyranga rubra.—The Scarlet Tanager.

This elegant bird is seven and four-tenths inches long; the wing, four inches; the color, bright scarlet, wings and tail black. Nests, on a low branch of a tree ; eggs, three to five ; dull, greenish-blue, speckled with reddish-brown and light purple. This is our most gaudy visitor. It arrives from the south about the fifteenth of May, and leaves early in September. This bird thrives well in confinement, and makes a beautiful pet. Feeds upon insects, berries, and grain.

Family BOMBYCILLIDÆ. *THE CHATTERERS.*

Sub-Family BOMBYCILLINÆ.—*The Wax Wings.*

BOHEMIAN CHATTERER.

Ampelis garrulus.—The Bohemian Chatterer.

This very rare and beautiful bird appears in Canada only in severe seasons. Length, seven and a-half inches ; the wing, four and a-half inches. The general color, brownish-ash ; primaries and tail feathers, plumbeous-black, the tail with a terminal band of yellow ; the head and throat marked with black ; the wings with white ; and the secondaries have red horny tips.

They live in numerous flocks, keeping by pairs only in the breeding season. Their food consists chiefly of the buds and seeds of the pine, cedar, and juniper. Their migrations extend from Central Asia to the Arctic regions. They breed in the northern part of British Columbia and Alaska.

A. cedrorum.—The Cedar Bird, or Cherry Bird.

The Cedar Birds arrive here in flocks about the second week in March. They generally build their nests in orchard trees ; sometimes in a cedar or other evergreen tree ; eggs, four or five in number, of a light blue or clay-white color, with a slight purple tint, with black spots. Farmers manifest a great deal of ill - feeling toward this bird, on account of its occasional fondness for cherries and other small fruit. It has, however, a much greater relish for caterpillars and the larvæ of insects, of which it destroys immense numbers, and thereby more than compensates for the small quantity of fruit it eats. The only note of the Cherry Bird is *twee-twee*, uttered in a plaintive, soft manner. The general color is reddish-olive above, passing into yellow beneath ; the quills and tail, dark plumbeous and dusky, tipped with yellow. The plumage is very soft and delicate, and its tints and shadings beautiful.

7

Family LANIIDÆ.

Sub-Family LANIINÆ.—*The Shrikes.*

GREAT NORTHERN SHRIKE.

Collyrio borealis.—The Great Northern Shrike, or
Butcher Bird.

The Butcher Bird is nine inches long; the
color, above, light bluish-ash; the under parts,
white; the wings and tail, black. It feeds principally upon insects, sparrows, and other small
birds. It can imitate the calls of other birds,
especially those indicating distress; and has the
cruel habit of impaling its prey on sharp twigs
and thorns, and devouring it at leisure. Hence,
it has derived the name, Butcher Bird. The
nest is usually built in a thorn tree or low
shrub; eggs, four or five in number; of a
dirty lead-colored white, with spots of brown
on the large end.

C. excubitorides.—The White-rumped Shrike.

The characteristics of this shrike are similar to those of the preceding species, except that the tail is shorter and the head larger.

Sub-Family VIREONINÆ.—*The Vireos.*

Vireo olivaceus.—The Red-eyed Vireo.

This is one of our most industrious and interesting little visitors. It is six and a-half inches long, the wing three and a-half inches. Color, olive-green, above; white, below; the head, dark ash ; and iris, red ; a whitish line from the bill over the eye. The nest is generally suspended from forked twigs; eggs, four to six, spotted with reddish-brown. Feeds entirely upon insects and their larvæ. The Red-eyed Vireo is one of the earliest singers of spring, and the latest of autumn. Its notes are loud, clear, and melodious. Throughout the day he hops from branch to branch, searching in the foliage for caterpillars and noxious larvæ, Arrives in Canada about the tenth of May, and departs for the south early in October.

V. gilvus.—The Warbling Vireo.

This pretty bird is five and a-half inches long; the color, olive-green, above ; beneath, white, tinged with yellow. Its song is very mellow and swect. The nest is pensile, and usually built in tall trees; eggs, six; white, with small red spots on the large end. Arrives here about the first of May, and leaves late in September.

V. noveboracensis.—The White-eyed Vireo.

This sweet songster frequents the thickest bushes. It arrives in Canada about the first of May, and remains until October. Color, bright olive-green, above; white, beneath; iris, white. Nests, in a brier or raspberry bush; eggs, four in number, reddish-brown. While in search of insects it sings merrily and sweetly.

V. flavifrons.—The Yellow-throated Vireo.

This is a beautiful and rather uncommon bird with us. It usually arrives here about the fifteenth of May. Color, olive-green above; throat and breast, bright sulphur yellow; the remaining under parts, white. It is quite impossible to say too much in favor of this sweet songster. The nest is built a few feet from the ground, and is a beautiful specimen of nest-building; the eggs are four in number, pure white, spotted with brown. .

V. solitarius.—The Solitary Vireo.

This beautiful and active fly-catcher is five inches in length. Color, above, olive-green;

underneath, white ; sides, yellowish-green ; top and sides of the head, bluish-ash. Breeds in Canada. Nests, in the topmost branches of a tree ; eggs, four, white.

FAMILY ALAUDIDÆ. *THE SKYLARKS.*

SHORE LARK.

Eremophila cornuta.—The Shore Lark.

The Shore Lark arrives in Canada late in the fall. Color, pinkish-brown ; the feathers of the back, marked with dusky-brown ; the frontal band and under parts, white ; neck and throat, yellow ; a crescentric patch from the bill below the eye, and along the side of the head, and a black pectoral crescent. While on the wing it sings sweetly. Its nest is always built on the ground ; eggs, four in number, of a faint

grayish-brown color. The Shore Lark is one of
our few winter birds ; in March it leaves for the
far north to breed.

FAMILY FRINGILLIDÆ.

Sub-Family COCCOTHRAUSTINÆ.—*The Finches.*

Pinicola canadensis.—The Pine Grosbeak.

This bird visits us during the severest seasons
only. Its habitat is the extreme northern part
of this continent. Large numbers visited this
section of Canada in the winter of 1867. The
Pine Grosbeak is eight and a-half inches long ;
beak, dusky, very thick at the base, and hooked,
at the tip ; head, neck, breast, and rump, rose-
colored crimson ; back, black ; greater wing-
coverts, tipped with white, forming two bars on
the wing ; quills, black, edged with white ; belly,
straw-colored. The female is brownish above,
greenish-yellow beneath ; the top of the head
and rump, brownish gamboge-yellow. Feeds
upon the small buds which shoot out from the
branches of the fir and other trees.

Carpodacus purpureus.—The Purple Finch.

The Purple Finch arrives here about the last
of April, in flocks of a dozen or more. It is six

and a-half inches long ; the color, crimson; belly and under tail coverts, white ; two thin reddish bands aross the wings. The female is olive-brown above, and white beneath. Its song is sweet and warbling. Nests, in a tree, a few feet from the ground ; eggs, four in number, of a bluish-green color. Its food consists principally of the buds and blossoms of fruit trees.

Chrysomitris tristis.—The Yellow Bird.

This is a well-known and common summer visitor. Color, bright yellow ; crown, wings, and tail, black. The nest is usually built in the branch of a tree, twenty feet from the ground ; eggs, four or five, white, tinged with blue, and spotted with reddish-brown. Arrives here in flocks early in May. In the fall its color is changed to a greenish-olive, resembling the female. About the last of September they gather in flocks and move southward.

C. pinus.—The Pine Finch.

The Pine Finch arrives in Canada late in the fall, and remains throughout the winter. It frequents the pine forests. Feeds on the seeds contained in the pine cones. Color, above, brownish-olive ; beneath, whitish, streaked with dusky brown ; tail, forked. Breeds north of Ontario.

Curvirostra americana.—The Red Crossbill.

The Red Crossbill is six inches long ; the color, dull red ; the wings and tail, blackish-brown. This bird is an inhabitant of the pine forests of the far north, and usually visits us during the winter. Its food consists of the seeds of the pine and hemlock, which it detaches from the cones and husks that enclose them with its peculiarly shaped bill, which is crossed.

Curvirostra leucoptera.—The White-winged Crossbill.

This bird has all the general characteristics of the Red Crossbill, but is readily distinguished by the white bands across the wings.

Ægiothus linaria.—The Lesser Red-poll.

This is a common winter visitor with us. It is four and a-half inches long ; the color, above, light yellowish, each feather streaked with dark brown ; the crown, crimson ; upper parts of the breast, tinged with light crimson ; white, underneath. Few birds manifest a more affectionate disposition than the little Red-poll. I have often seen a dozen or more sitting on a branch, feeding each other, and exhibiting other marks of kindness and affection. This bird breeds in the arctic regions.

Plectrophanes nivales.—The Snow Bunting.

This is another very common winter visitor in this part of Canada. They move in large flocks, and are sometimes accompanied by Red-polls and Shore Larks. Color, above, black and white; underneath, white; head and rump, yellowish-brown. They breed in Lapland and other parts of the far north.

P. Lapponicus.—Lapland Bunting.

This Bunting breeds in Lapland. Head and neck, black, with a red crescent on the hind neck; rest of upper parts, black; lower parts, white. Visits Canada during the fall migrations.

Sub-Family SPIZELLINÆ.—*The Sparrows.*

Passerculus savanna.—The Savannah Sparrow.

This sparrow arrives here about the middle of April. Is five and a-half inches long; the upper parts streaked with dark brown, the crown with a medium stripe of yellowish-gray; eyelids, yellow; the forepart of the breast, streaked; the under parts white. Nests on the ground; eggs, four to six, pale blue, mottled with purplish-brown. Departs for the south early in October. All the birds of this family feed upon insects and seeds. Two broods are raised in a season. It is a fine singer.

8

Poocætes gramineus.—The Bay-winged Bunting.

The Bay-winged Bunting is six and a-quarter inches long ; above, yellowish-brown ; the feathers streaked abruptly with dark brown ; beneath, yellowish-white ; the breast and belly streaked with brown ; the wings, light chestnut-brown. Nests, on the ground ; eggs, four to six, bluish-white, with reddish-brown blotches. It arrives the first week in April, and leaves for the south the last of September. The Bay-winged Bunting sings, for an hour at a time, in a sweet, tender strain.

Coturniculus passerinus.—The Yellow-winged Sparrow.

This sparrow arrives in Ontario about the first week in May, and leaves early in September. It is about five inches long ; the feathers above, brownish-rufous ; the crown, black, with a yellowish-brown stripe ; the end of the wing, bright yellow ; the lower parts are brownish-yellow. Nests, on the ground ; eggs, six, dull white, sprinkled with brown. Two broods are raised in the same season.

Zonotrichia leucophrys.—The White-crowned Sparrow.

This bird visits us during the spring and autumn migrations. It arrives here from the

south about the middle of May, and returns
from the north, where it breeds, in October.
The song of the White-crowned Sparrow is
clear, musical, and plaintive. This bird is over
seven inches long, the wing three and a-quarter
inches; the head above the upper half of the
loral region, and a line through and behind the
eye to the occiput, black; a patch upon the
crown, white; general color, pale ash above,
and white beneath. Feeds on insects, seeds,
and berries.

Z. albicollis.—The White-throated Sparrow.

The White-throated Sparrow is seven inches
long; the crown with two black stripes, separated by one of white; a broad yellow stripe to
the middle of the eye, and white behind it;
upper part of breast, dark ash; edge of wing,
yellow; the back, rufous-brown; the belly, and
two bands across the wings, white. This beautiful sparrow arrives in Ontario about the first
of May. Its song is indescribably sweet and
musical. I have frequently heard it at night,
when passing through the woods. Its food consists of seeds, berries, and insects. They collect
in small flocks about the middle of October,
and leave for the south. Nests, on the ground;
eggs, four, grayish-white.

Junco hyemalis.—The Snow Bird.

The general color of this bird is grayish or ashy-black ; the breast, belly, and second external tail feathers, white ; the third tail feather, white, margined with black. Length, six inches. This well-known bird arrives here in large flocks during the winter, and is quite tame. Their migrations extend from the arctic circle to the Gulf of Mexico. Numbers of these birds remain here through the summer ; they build their nests in stumps, or in a clump of moss ; eggs, white, spotted with reddish-brown and grayish-white. There is a widespread impression that the Snow Bird of winter is the Chipping Sparrow of the summer. I am satisfied it is a mistake. The Chipping Sparrow differs in plumage and size from the Snow Bird.

Spizella monticola.—The Tree Sparrow.

The Tree Sparrow is six and a-quarter inches long ; the feathers of the back, dark brown centrally, then rufous, edged with white. The head, chestnut ; the under parts are white, with a blotch of brown on the chest. This bird breeds in the northern forests.

S. pusilla.—The Field Sparrow.

The Field Sparrow arrives here about the twentieth of April. Inhabits the pastures and low woods. General color, rufous red, the under parts white, tinged before with yellow. Nests, upon the ground ; eggs, four in number, of a grayish-white, with blotches of lavender. The Field Sparrows collect in flocks about the first of September, and leave for the south.

S. sociallis.—The Chipping Sparrow.

This is one of our most common sparrows. It arrives here the last of March, and leaves for the south in October. It is five and a-half inches long. Rump, back of neck, and sides of neck and head, ashy ; crown, chestnut ; forehead, black, separated in middle by white ; a white streak over the eye ; the under parts, white. Builds its nest in low bushes ; eggs, four in number, greenish-blue, with dark brown spots. Feeds upon seeds, berries, and insects.

Melospiza melodia.—The Song Sparrow.

The Song Sparrow is rufous-brown above ; the under parts, white ; the breast and sides of the body and throat, streaked with dark rufous. This sparrow is one of our most common birds, and one of the sweetest songsters of the sparrow family. It makes its appearance here about the middle of March. The nest is usually built on the ground, or in a low bush ; eggs, four or five in number, bluish-white, and variously marked. Two broods are raised in the season.

M. palustris.—The Swamp Sparrow.

This sparrow arrives from the south about the middle of April. It prefers low, swampy localities, and is seldom seen in the open fields. This sparrow is six inches long; the crown, chestnut; forehead, black; ash-colored streak on the side of the head and back; under parts, whitish, tinged with ashy. The nest is built at the foot of a tuft of long grass; eggs, four in number, grayish-white, spotted with brown. Its food is grass-seeds, berries, and insects. The Swamp Sparrow has no song. Departs for the south about the tenth of October.

Sub-Family PASSERELLINÆ.—*The Buntings.*

Passerella iliaca.—The Fox-colored Sparrow.

This sparrow is seven and a-half inches long. Head, neck, rump, and middle of the back, dull ash color; each feather blotched with brownish-red; the tail, bright rufous; the under parts of the breast, sides, and throat, spotted with rufous. Nests, under a low bush; eggs, four or five, of a greenish color, with blotches of brown.

Sub-Family SPIZINÆ.

Emberiza americana.—The Black-throated
Bunting.

The Black-throated Bunting is a rare spring
visitor.   Length, six and a-half inches ; sides of
the head, and sides and back of the neck, ash ;
middle of the breast, yellow ; under parts, white,
with a black patch upon the throat.   Breeds in
Pennsylvania and Virginia.

ROSE-BREASTED GROSBEAK.

Guiraca ludoviciana.—The Rose-breasted
Grosbeak.

The Rose-breasted Grosbeak arrives in Canada
about the first of May, and remains until October,
when it goes south.   General color, above, glossy

black ; a broad carmine crescent across the breast, auxiliaries, and under wing coverts ; the rest of the under parts, white. The song of this beautiful and solitary bird is mellow, plaintive, and loud. Perched upon the topmost branches of a tree in the thickest of the wood, it wafts forth its tender and affecting song for hours at a time. Its food consists of berries and buds. The nest is often built in a low shrub or tree ; eggs, three or four in number, of a greenish-blue color, covered with fine spots of umber-brown.

G. cærula.—The Blue Grosbeak.

The prevailing color of this extremely beautiful and graceful bird is a brilliant blue. Length, seven and a-half inches. Habitat, British Columbia, Manitoba, and the extreme western part of the United States. A very rare visitor in Canada.

Coccothraustes vespertina.—The Evening Grosbeak.

This Grosbeak is another rare visitor from the western part of this continent. Head and neck, black; remaining upper parts, yellow; abdomen, yellowish-olive ; bill, stout.

C. cardinalis.—Cardinal, or Red Bird.

The general color of this gaudy bird is ver- million ; a black band around the upper part of the throat and the base of the bill. Length, eight and three-quarter inches. Habitat, Virginia and the Carolinas. Occurs very rarely in Canada.

Cyanospiza cyanea.—The Indigo Bird.

This beautiful bird is five and a-half inches long. The color, bright ultra-marine blue ; wing feathers tinged with dull bluish-brown. This bird prefers the skirts of the forests. Its song is sweet and interesting. Nests, in low bushes ; eggs, six ; color, blue, with purple spots. It arrives from the south about the twentieth of May, and returns late in September. Feeds on insects and berries.

Pipilo erythropthalmus.—The Ground Robin, or Chewink.

This is a common visitor. It arrives in the vicinity of Toronto about the twentieth of May; the males arriving about ten days before the females. For two or three hours after sunrise, the Chewink sits perched upon the top of a small tree or bush, and sings with mellow sweetness, which cannot fail to interest the hearer. Nests, on the ground, beneath a tuft of grass ; eggs, four in number, of a flesh color, with dark spots. Two broods, and sometimes three, are raised in the season. They collect in flocks about the last of October, and leave for the south.

9

THE BOBOLINK.

FAMILY ICTERIDÆ.

Sub-Family AGELAEINÆ.—*The Starlings.*

Dolichonyx oryzivorus.—The Bobolink.

This well-known and beautiful bird arrives in Canada about the last of May. Length, seven and three-quarter inches. Color, black, beautifully marked with cream color and white. The female is yellowish beneath ; above, dark brown. The male assumes the color of the female in the fall. Its cheerful, loud, and jingling song is heard in every meadow in the summer, from morning until evening. Nests, on the ground ; eggs, four to six, of a light ashy-blue color, with

spots of dark brown. This bird feeds on insects
and seeds. Early in September they collect in
large flocks and move southward.

Molothrus pecoris.—The Cow Bird.

The Cow Bird is eight inches long. The
breast, neck, and lower half of the breast, light
brown ; the rest of the body, bright black.
During the summer, this bird frequents pasture
fields, where cattle are grazing. It builds no
nest, but secretly deposits its eggs in the nests
of other birds—usually in the nest of a Sparrow
or Blue Bird. It lays but one egg in each nest,
of a light grayish-blue, with brown spots. The
Cow Bird feeds on insects principally. About
the last of October they collect in large flocks,
and leave for the south.

Agelaius phœniceus.—The Red-winged
Black Bird.

This bird arrives here in small flocks about the
last of March. General color, lustrous black ;
the shoulders, vermillion or bright crimson.
Nests, in a low bush in a swamp or meadow ;
eggs, four in number, of a light blue color,
marked with brown spots. About the twentieth
of October the Red-winged Black Birds collect
in large flocks, and leave for their southern home.
Their food consists of the seeds of aquatic grasses
and grain, of which they are extremely fond, to
the injury of the farmer.

MEADOW LARK.

Sturnella magna.—The Meadow Lark.

The Meadow Lark is one of our most common and beautiful summer visitors. It arrives here about the fifteenth of March. General color, above, dark brown, with streaks of brownish-white ; beneath, yellow, with a black pectoral crescent. Nests, on the ground ; eggs, four or five, pure white, slightly sprinkled with reddish-brown blotches. Its food consists principally of insects, worms, beetles, and grass seeds. Leaves for the south about the first of November.

Sub-Family ICTERINÆ.—*The Orioles.*

Icterus spurius.—The Orchard Oriole.

The Orchard Oriole is seven and a-quarter inches long ; the head, neck, and tail, black ; under parts, brownish-chestnut ; a narrow white line across the wings. Nests, in orchard trees or upon willows ; eggs, four to six, bluish-white, sprinkled with dark brown. This oriole is a rare visitor in Ontario. Feeds upon fruit, caterpillars, and insects.

I. baltimore.—The Baltimore Oriole, or Golden Robin.

This beautiful and well-known bird is one of our regular summer visitors. It arrives here about the middle of May. General color, black; the rump, upper tail coverts, lesser wing coverts, the terminal portion of all but two tail feathers, and the under parts, orange-red ; the edges of quills, and a band across the tip of the greater coverts, white. The nest of this oriole is a beautiful piece of nest-architecture, and is usually constructed on the outer drooping twigs of elm or orchard trees ; it is a pendulous cylindric pouch, of six or seven inches in depth; eggs, four or five, of a flesh color. The song of this beautiful bird is loud, full, and mellow. About the middle of September the Golden Robin leaves for the south.

Sub-Family QUISCALINÆ.—*The Grackles.*

Scolecophagus ferrugineus.—The Rusty Grackle.

This bird arrives here about the last of March, and retires to the low swampy thickets surrounding marshes. General color, black, with purple reflections. Nests, in low bushes near the water ; eggs, four, bluish-white. It feeds upon the seeds of aquatic grasses, insects, and worms.

Quiscalus versicolor.—The Purple Grackle.

The Purple Grackle arrives in Ontario about the middle of April. General color, steel-blue, with varied reflections of purple and bronze. Nests, in a tree in or near a marsh or pond ; eggs, four, light brown. Food consists of grubs, worms, and grains. These birds prove very injurious to the farmers in the fall, as they collect in large flocks, and visit the corn-fields, destroying great quantities of grain.

FAMILY CORVIDÆ.

Sub-Family CORVINÆ.—*The Crows.*

Corvus americanus.—The Crow.

This bird has a very unenviable notoriety. It is an enemy to the farmer, and very destructive to small birds, as it feeds upon their young. Agricultural societies should offer a premium for its destruction.

Corvus corax.—The Raven.

This interesting bird has become very rare in Canada. A few specimens are occasionally seen in the vicinity of Niagara Falls and the Welland Canal. The Raven is twenty-six inches in length; the bill is large and strong; the plumage, deep glossy black. This species is found in every part of the world. Its food consists of dead animal matter, and, like the common crow, it devours the eggs and young of other birds.

Sub-Family GARRULINÆ.—*The Jays.*

BLUE JAY.

Cyanurus cristatus.—The Blue Jay.

This elegant bird often remains in this section of Canada throughout the year. It is, without exception, our most beautiful bird. The head is handsomely crested, with loose silky plumes; bill, black; legs, brown; the whole bird is of a fine blue color, the under parts, with the wings and tail, marked by bars; neck, encircled with black ring. It has the cruel habit of destroying the young of other birds. Its nest is usually built in a small cedar or pine tree ; eggs, four in number, of a light green color, spotted with brown. The Blue Jay is one of the noisiest birds of our forests, its notes being discordant and harsh.

Perisoreus canadensis.—The Canada Jay.

This Jay is a rare visitor in Ontario. Its habitat is Labrador and eastern Canada. Nests, in a fir-tree ; eggs, four, of a light gray color. The head, neck, and breast, are white ; rest of upper parts, ashy-plumbeous ; beneath, light gray. It resembles the Blue Jay in motions and note, and is equally rapacious and destructive.

ORDER IV.—Rasores. (Scratchers.)

SUB-ORDER COLUMBÆ.

FAMILY COLUMBIDÆ. *THE DOVES.*

Sub-Family COLUMBINÆ.

Ectopistes migratoria.—The Wild Pigeon.

This well-known bird is a resident of Canada, except in the most severe cold weather. Its migrations are made solely to obtain food. They pass from one section of the continent to another in immense flocks. The nests are usually built in the forked branch of a tree. I have often seen thirty or forty nests in one tree. The eggs are two in number, pure white, with a slight red tint. Feeds upon grain and seeds.

Zenaidura carolinensis.—The Carolina Dove.

The Carolina Dove is an irregular summer visitor in Canada. Color, above, blue, overlaid with olive-brown ; under parts, light reddish-brown ; breast, purplish-red ; bill, black ; feet, yellow. This dove sits upon the ground during the night. Nests, in a tree ; eggs, two in number, pure white.

10

SUB-ORDER GALLINÆ.

FAMILY TETRAONIDÆ. *THE GROUSE.*

Tetrao canadensis.—The Canada Grouse, or Spruce Partridge.

This well-known bird is a permanent resident, and may be found in large numbers in the back settlements of Canada. It is stately and graceful in its movements. General color of the head, neck, and body of the male bird is transversely barred with dusky and gray brown; over the eyelids is a bare red space; nostrils covered with black, with a small white spot on each side, and one beneath; throat, breast, and belly, black; the latter spotted with white, except the middle; sides of the body barred transversely with gray-brown and dusky; the feathers with a white stripe near the tip; under tail coverts, black and white; tail, black, tipped with rufous; feathers of the tarsi, gray-brown; claws, gray; beak, black. Nests, upon the ground; eggs, eight or ten in number, of a light buff, with brown spots.

RUFFLED GROUSE.

Bonasa umbellus.—The Ruffled Grouse, or Partridge.

This Partridge is a permanent resident of Canada. It is often found in the open woods and evergreen thickets in well settled districts. When walking it struts with a haughty step, elevating its ruff, and spreading its pretty tail. The habits of this Partridge are solitary; it is seldom found in coveys of more than six or eight together. General color, above, reddish-brown; the back, with light brown; beneath, white, barred with dull brown; the feathers of the ruff, black; tail, grayish, with a black bar near the end. Nests, upon the ground, at the foot of a bush, or under an old log; eggs, eight to twelve, of a yellow-white color.

Tetrao phasianellus.—The Sharp-tailed Grouse.

Habitat, British Columbia and Manitoba. Accidental in Canada. Color, above, yellowish-red and brownish-black ; throat, reddish-white, with dusky spots ; breast and sides, covered with dusky spots ; abdomen, white.

FAMILY PERDICIDÆ.

Sub-Family ORTYGINÆ.

Ortyx virginianus.—The Virginia Partridge, or Quail.

The Virginia Partridge is brownish-red, above ; underneath, white ; the head marked with white and black. Length, ten inches. Nests on the ground ; eggs, white, ten or more in number. This beautiful Partridge has become almost extinct in Canada. It is often called "*Bob White,*" on account of its peculiar cry.

FAMILY PHASIANIDÆ.

Meleagris gallopavo.—The Wild Turkey.

This magnificent fowl is a permanent resident of Canada. Color, copper-bronze, with green reflections, each feather with a black margin ; tail, chestnut, barred with black ; head, livid-blue, and the legs, red. In other respects it resembles the domestic turkey. The great beauty and size of this bird, and the fact of its being the origin of all the domestic varieties, render it a most interesting species.

ORDER V.—Grallatores. (Waders.)

SUB-ORDER HERODIONES.

FAMILY ARDEIDÆ. *THE HERONS.*

GREAT BLUE HERON.

Ardea herodias.—The Great Blue Heron.

The Great Blue Heron is a regular summer visitor in Canada.   It usually arrives here about the twentieth of April, and remains until the tenth or fifteenth of October, when it leaves for the south. The general color of this heron is a delicate gray; throat and neck, white, with patches of dark bluish-gray; a black line over the eye; a pendant tuft at the junction of the neck and breast; a long plume of a bluish-black color. This bird is extremely shy, and is approached with difficulty. It frequents marshes and the borders of lakes and rivers, and feeds upon reptiles and fishes. When standing erect the Great Blue Heron will measure from four and a-half to five feet; its beak is seven to eight inches in length, very strong, and can be used with terrible force as an offensive weapon. The nest of this bird is usually built in the top of a large tree; eggs, four or five, of a pale green color.

Ardetta exilis.—The Least Bittern.

This bird is a frequent summer visitor to the marsh, east of Toronto. It is solitary and nocturnal in its habits. General color, dark green, above, and purplish-brown on the sides and underneath. Length, thirteen inches; wing, four and a-half inches. Nests, in low bushes on the margin of ponds or marshes; eggs, four in number, of a greenish-yellow color. Feeds upon small reptiles and fish.

GREAT BITTERN.

Botaurus lentiginosus.—The Great Bittern,
or Stake Driver.

The Great Bittern arrives in Canada about the
middle of April, and remains until late in October. The general color of this bittern is a rich
brownish-buff, covered with streaks and mottlings
of black, brown, gray, and chestnut. Nests, on
marshy ground ; eggs, four or five, pale brown.
Its food consists of reptiles and insects.

Butorides virescens.—The Green Heron.

The Green Heron is eighteen inches long ;
above, dark green ; wings and tail, green ; legs,
yellow ; belly, ashy-brown ; head, has a crest of

glossy-green feathers. This Heron is occasionally seen in Canada in the spring. Nests, in trees in swampy woods ; eggs, four in number ; of a pale light blue color. Feeds upon crabs, frogs, and worms.

Nyctiardea Gardenii.—The Night Heron.

The Night Heron arrives in the vicinity of Toronto about the fifteenth or twentieth of April. General color, above, steel-green ; wings and tail, ashy-blue ; under parts and sides, a lilac color. Length, twenty inches ; the bill is slightly arched, strong, and black. During the day this bird is often seen perched upon the top of a tall tree in a swamp, but when night approaches it begins its flight in pursuit of food, which consists principally of insects, frogs, lizards, and fish. The nest of the Night Heron is built in a tree ; eggs, four ; of a greenish-yellow color.

FAMILY GRUIDÆ. *THE CRANES.*

Grus canadensis.—The Sandhill Crane.

The Sandhill Crane is an accidental visitor ; a few specimens are occasionally seen during the spring and autumn migrations. Breeds in Manitoba and British Columbia. Length, fifty inches ; beak, four inches ; top of the head covered with a red skin ; neck, gray ; belly, breast, sides, and thighs, ash color ; tail, deep ash color ; legs and bare part of the thigh, black.

Grus americana.—The White Crane.

This magnificent bird occasionally visits Western Canada. It is fifty-two inches in length ; the plumage, pure white. Its migrations extend from South America to the arctic circle.

Ibis falcinellus.—The Glossy Ibis.

This beautiful bird is an accidental visitor. Head, glossy green, with purple reflections; neck, back, breast, and abdomen, dark chestnut ; part of breast shaded with green ; sides, dusky, tinged with green ; edge of wings, dark red, upper parts, dark green, glossed with purple. Breeds in Virginia and Florida.

·SUB-ORDER GRALLÆ.

FAMILY CHARADRIDÆ. *THE PLOVERS.*

Charadrius virginicus.—The Golden Plover.

This Plover passes through Canada about the last of April, on its way north to breed. About the first of September, they again visit Canada in small flocks while migrating southward. Color, above, brownish-black, with irregular spots of golden-yellow ; beneath, black, with lustrous brown. Nests, in the grass; eggs, four, of a light buff color.

11

Ægialitis vociferus.—The Kill-deer Plover.

The Kill-deer Plover is a summer resident of Canada.   Color, above, light brown ; rump, rufous ; black band on the breast ; and around the neck a black ring ; beneath, white.   It is called "*Kill-deer*," from its note.   Nests, on the ground ; eggs, four, light buff color.

Æ. montanus.—The Mountain Plover.

The Mountain Plover is an accidental visitor in Canada.   Length, nine inches.   Color, grayish-brown.   Breeds in Manitoba and British Columbia.

Æ. Wilsonius.—Wilson's Plover.

This bird is occasionally met with in Canada late in the fall.   Breeds in Delaware, Virginia, and the Carolinas.   Color, ashy-brown above, the feathers edged with pale ashy ; band on the breast, brownish-black ; bill, black ; legs, yellow. Length, eight inches.

Æ. semi-palmatus.—Semi-palmated Plover.

This Plover breeds north of Ontario.   Spring and fall visitor.   Color, above, light ashy-brown ; beneath, white.   Length, seven inches.

Æ. melodus.—The Piping Plover.

The Piping Plover arrives from the south about the last of April.   It is a regular summer visitor in Canada. Color, above, light brown ; beneath, white ; length, eight inches. Nests, in the sand ; eggs, four, light buff.

Squatarola helvetica.—The Black-bellied Plover.

This Plover breeds north of Ontario. Arrives in Canada in September, in flocks. In their habits they closely resemble the Golden Plover. Color, above, white ; beneath, black ; sides of the neck and rump, ashy ; bill and legs, black. Length, eleven and a-half inches.

Family HÆMATOPIDIDÆ. *THE OYSTER-CATCHERS.*

Hæmatopus palliatus.—The Oyster-catchers.

This species is a rare visitor in Canada. Head, neck, upper part of breast, quill feathers, and latter half of tail feathers, deep shining black : the rest of the plumage is pure white ; bill, three inches long, and flattened sideways.

H. niger.—Backman's Oyster-catcher.

The general color of this bird is dark brown ; head and breast, brownish-black. It is occasionally shot, in the fall, on the island opposite Toronto.

Strepsilas interpres.—The Turnstone.

The Turnstone breeds in Manitoba. Visits Canada in small numbers in the spring and fall. Color, black, rufous, and white, above ; abdomen, white ; head and neck, marked with stripes of brownish-black.

S. melanocephala.—The Black Turnstone.

This species is an accidental visitor. Color, · darker than the preceding. Length, eleven inches.

FAMILY RECURVIROSTRIDÆ. *THE AVOSETS.*

Recurvirostra americana.—The American Avoset.

The Avoset is quite accidental in Canada. On the shores of the Caspian and the salt lakes of Tartary they are very abundant. Specimens have been shot late in the fall on the island, opposite Toronto. Length, seventeen inches ; The head and neck, pale reddish-brown ; back and quills, black ; other parts, white. The bill, which is three inches long, turns up like a hook, and is flat, thin, and sharp.

FAMILY PHALAROPODIDÆ. *THE PHALAROPES.*

Phalaropus hyperboreus.—The Northern Phalarope.

The Northern Phalarope is an occasional spring and fall visitor in Canada. Breeds in

Manitoba ; nests, on the ground ; eggs, four in number, of a brownish-drab color. This beautiful little bird is a swimmer as well as a wader : its motions, while swimming and wading, are exceedingly graceful and interesting. The migrations of this species extend from Manitoba to the Gulf of Mexico. Head and neck, sooty-ash color; wings, back, and tail, brownish-black ; abdomen, white ; legs and bill, dark ; throat and breast, white ; and the neck, with a ring of bright ferruginous.

P. Wilsonii.—Wilson's Phalarope.

Wilson's Phalarope is also an occasional visitor in Canada. Color, dark above ; white, beneath ; a stripe of bright reddish-brown around the neck, running upwards to the back.

P. fulicarius.—The Red Phalarope.

Several specimens of this rare and beautiful bird have been shot near Toronto this fall. General color, deep slate, streaked with brownish-yellow, and reddish-chocolate.

FAMILY SCOLOPACIDÆ. *THE SNIPES.*

Philohela minor.—The Woodcock.

This well-known bird arrives here early in March. Color, above, variegated with reddish-black and ashy ; underneath, rufous ; legs, pale red ; bill, dark brown. Nests, on the ground, beneath a log or bush ; eggs, four ; of a yellow-ish-drab color, with dark brown blotches.　Early in November the Woodcock leaves for the south.

WILSON'S SNIPE.

Gallinago Wilsonii.—Wilson's Snipe.

Wilson's Snipe is a well-known summer visitor in Canada.　It arrives about the tenth of March. Feeds upon earthworms principally.　Nests, on the ground ; eggs, four, of an olive-drab color, slightly marked with brown spots.　General color, above, brownish-black, marked with light rufous, yellowish-brown, or ashy-white ;　underneath, white.　Late in the fall this snipe goes south.

Macrorhamphus griseus.—The Gray Snipe.

The Gray Snipe is dark-ashy above ; pale reddish and black on the back ; rump and upper tail coverts, white ; under parts, pale red and brownish-black. This snipe arrives here about the twentieth of April. Breeds in the north, and again visits Canada about the first of September.

M. scolopaceus.—The Greater Longbeak.

This snipe is an irregular visitor in Canada. Length, twelve inches ; color, above, brownish-black, and yellow ; beneath, wood-brown, with spots of umber.

Sub-Family TRINGINÆ.—*The Sandpipers,*

Tringa canutus.—The Gray-back, or Robin Snipe.

The Gray-back is a spring and fall visitor. It is the largest of the Sandpipers. Upper parts, light gray, with irregular spots of black ; under parts, light reddish-brown. Breeds in the north.

T. Cooperii.—Cooper's Sandpiper.

This Sandpiper occasionally visits Canada during the spring and fall migrations.

T. maritima.—The Purple Sandpiper.

This pretty bird is frequently seen in Canada in the fall. Breeds in the far north. Head and upper parts, smoky-brown, with a purple tinge ; under parts, white.

T. subarquata.—The Curlew Sandpiper.

The Curlew Sandpiper is a very rare visitor in Canada. Upper parts, brownish-black, spotted with bright yellowish-red ; under parts, dark yellowish-rufous.

T. alpina.—The Red-backed Sandpiper.

This species visits Canada during the spring and autumn in large numbers. Upper parts, dark ash color ; abdomen, white ; breast, pale ash, with streaks of brown.

T. maculata.—The Jack Snipe.

The Jack Snipe is a regular spring and fall vititor, usually arriving in Canada early in May and about the middle of September. It is commonly called " Grass Bird," by which name it is generally known.

T. Wilsonii.—The Least Sandpiper, or Peep.

This Sandpiper is the smallest of the family. It arrives in Canada about the middle of May, and soon leaves for the interior of the country, where it breeds.

T. Bonapartii.—Bonaparte's Sandpiper.

Bonaparte's Sandpiper is light ashy-brown, above ; darker on the rump ; under parts, white. Arrives here in small flocks during the spring and fall migrations.

Calidris arenaria.—The Sanderling, or Beach-bird.

The Sanderling breeds in Manitoba. It has all the characteristics of the Sandpipers. Upper parts, light ashy; under parts, pure white; no hind toe; front toes rather long; bill, straight and rather thick. It visits Canada in small flocks early in September.

Ereunetes petrificatus.—The Semi-palmated Sandpiper.

This Sandpiper is six and a-half inches in length, and has the feet semi-palmated. In other respects it resembles the Least Sandpiper. Breeds in Manitoba. It is accidental in Canada.

Micropalma himantopus.—The Stilt Sandpiper.

The Stilt Sandpiper is an occasional visitor during the fall migrations.

Sub-Family TOTANINÆ.—*The Stilts.*

Symphemia semipalmata.—The Willet.

The Willet is dark ashy above; rump and under parts, white. Breeds in Canada. Nests, on the sandy beach of an island; eggs, four in number, of a pale olive color.

12

Gambetta melanoleuca.—The Greater Yellow-legs, or Tell-tale.

This species breeds in Manitoba. Visits Canada in the spring and fall. Entire upper parts of the body, cinereous ; under parts, white ; neck and legs, long ; legs, yellow.

G. flavipes.—The Yellow-legs.

The Yellow-legs is well-known in Canada as a spring and fall visitor. It is smaller than the preceding bird. Breeds in the northern part of this continent.

Rhyacophilus solitarius.—The Solitary Sandpiper.

The Solitary Sandpiper is frequently called "Wagtail," from its habit of nodding its head and tipping up its tail. Remains in Canada through the summer. Upper parts, greenish-brown, with spots of ashy-white ; under parts, white ; bill, curved upward from the middle.

Tringoides macularius.—The Spotted Sandpiper.

The Spotted Sandpiper arrives in Canada in large flocks early in April, and remains through the summer. Nests, in the sand ; eggs, four in number, of a yellowish-buff color. Upper parts, brownish-olive-green, with irregular spots of brownish-black ; under parts, white.

Actiturus Bartramius.—The Field Plover.

The Field Plover breeds in Canada. Frequents grain fields and meadows. Upper parts brownish-black, with a greenish lustre ; under parts, pale yellowish-white ; middle tail feathers, greenish-brown ; legs, light yellow. Nests, on the ground ; eggs, four, of a creamy-drab color.

Tryngites rufescens.—The Buff-breasted Sandpiper.

This species is frequently seen in Canada during the fall migration. Breeds in the arctic regions. Legs, long ; upper parts, pale ashy-brown, with a yellowish tinge ; under parts, light yellowish-red.

Limosa fedoa.—The Marbled Godwit.

The Marbled Godwit is a spring and autumn visitor. Bill, long, curved upwards ; wings, long ; tail, short ; legs, long ; upper parts, brownish-black and pale reddish ; under parts, pale rufous, with lines of brownish-black.

L. hudsonica.—The Hudsonian Godwit.

This bird is an irregular fall visitor. Color, brownish-black above ; underneath, yellowish-red ; feathers, tipped with white ; length, eighteen inches ; bill, three inches.

LONG-BILLED CURLEW.

Numenius longirostris.—The Long-billed Curlew.

The Long-billed Curlew is a regular spring and fall visitor in Canada. Bill, very long, and curved downwards ; upper parts, pale rufous, with lines of black on the neck and sides ; legs, bluish-brown.

N. hudsonicus.—The Short-billed Curlew.

The Short-billed Curlew is also a spring and fall visitor. Bill, smaller than the preceding ; head, above, brownish-black ; other upper parts, brownish-black, tinged with ashy.

N. borealis.—The Esquimaux Curlew.

This Curlew is not often seen in Canada, as it merely remains for a few days during the spring and fall migrations. They breed in the far north. It is easily distinguished from the other two by its smaller size, and its small and weak bill.

Sub-Family RALLINÆ.—*The Rails.*

Rallus elegans.—The Marsh Hen.

The Marsh Hen occasionally visits Canada in the spring and autumn. Upper parts, olive-brown; underneath, chestnut.

R. crepitans.—The Clapper Rail.

The Clapper Rail is a summer resident of Canada. Color, above, light ashy-olive; neck and breast, tawny; abdomen and sides, brownish-black. Nests, on the ground, in or near a marsh; eggs, seven, of a creamy-drab color.

R. virginianus.—The Virginia Rail.

This species visits Canada in the spring, and remains until September. Upper parts, olive-brown, with stripes of brownish-black; throat, white; breast, bright rufous. Nests, in low meadows; eggs, eight, of a deep buff color. Food consists of insects and worms.

Porzana carolina.—The Carolina Rail.

The Carolina Rail arrives in Canada about the tenth of April, and frequents the marshes and meadows. Upper parts, greenish-brown, with bands of black; the sides of the neck and breast, bluish-ash; bill, greenish-yellow; legs, green. Nests, on the ground; eggs, eight in number, of a yellow-drab color, with an olive-tint. In October, or early in November, this species collect in flocks and leave for the coasts of Florida and Louisiana.

P. jamaicensis.—The Little Black Rail.

This pretty little Rail is an occasional fall visitor in Canada. Length, five inches. Color, blackish-brown.

P. noveboracensis.—The Yellow Rail.

This bird is a summer resident of Canada. Nests, in the grass; eggs, fourteen or fifteen, pure white. The upper parts are yellow-ochre color, with stripes of brownish-black; neck and breast, reddish-yellow; abdomen, white.

Crex pratensis.—The Corn Crake.

The Corn Crake is accidental in Canada. Color, blackish-brown. Length, ten inches. Bill, greenish-black.

Fulica americana.—The Coot.

The Coot is fourteen inches long. Upper parts, dark slate color, with an olive tint on the back and rump; head, black; abdomen, white. Breeds in Canada. Nests, in a bog, or near a muddy pond; eggs, twelve, of a light buff color.

PURPLE GALLINULE.

Gallinule martinica.—The Purple Gallinule.

The Purple Gallinule is twelve inches long. Upper parts, dark olive-green ; bill, bright red, tipped with yellow ; under parts, bluish-purple ; legs, yellow. An occasional visitor to the marsh, east of Toronto.

ORDER VI.—𝕬natatores. (𝕾wimmers.)

SUB-ORDER ANSERES.

Sub-Family CYGNINÆ.—The Swans.

Cygnus americanus.—The American Swan.

This magnificent bird is rare in the eastern part of Canada ; in the west it is occasionally met with in the vicinity of the river St. Clair. Several beautiful specimens were obtained near Goderich in the summer of 1870. The adult bird is pure white ; the bill and legs, black ; the tail has twenty feathers. The young birds are brown, with a reddish tint. Breeds in the north-west. Nests, on the ground ; eggs, eight in number, of an olive-green color. This swan is fifty-four inches long.

C. buccinator.—The Trumpeter Swan.

This beautiful swan is an accidental visitor, rarely seen east of Toronto. It is sixty-two inches long. Pure white ; the bill and legs, black. Its notes are loud and sonorous. Breeds in the north-west.

Sub-Family ANSERINÆ.—*The Geese.*

Anser hyperboreus.—The Snow Goose.

The Snow Goose is an occasional visitor in Canada. It is two feet eight inches in length, and its extended wings are five feet. The bill of this bird is very curious, the edges having each strong projecting teeth ; and the tongue, which is horny at the extremity, is armed on each side with thirteen long and sharp teeth. The upper mandible is bright red ; the lower, white. The head, neck, and body of the adult bird are pure white ; the quills are white for half their length, the rest, black ; the legs are deep red. The Snow Goose inhabits the arctic regions, occasionally migrating to Canada and the more temperate climes of Virginia and Maryland.

A. Gambelli.—The White-fronted Goose.

The White-fronted Goose is an accidental visitor. It is smaller than the Snow Goose. Color, grayish ; forehead, white ; bill and legs, red. The tail has sixteen feathers. Breeds in the far north.

A. frontalis.—The Brown-fronted Goose.

The Brown-fronted Goose is occasionally seen in Canada. It inhabits the frozen regions of the

13

north.   It resembles the White-fronted Goose in general appearance.   The forehead, however, is dark brown instead of white.

CANADA GOOSE.

Bernicla canadensis.—The Canada Goose, or Wild Goose.

The Canada Goose is a well known spring and fall visitor, passing here in flocks, in March or April, for the northern part of this continent, where it breeds, and remains until the hard frosts begin, when they leave for a more temperate climate.   Immense flocks of these geese can be seen almost daily on their way to the south, during the last of October and through the month of November. Each flock is usually attended by an old gander, who every now and then calls out his well known "*honk*," which is replied to by several members of the flock. The Canada Goose is thirty-five inches long. The upper parts, brownish ; the lower, a pale brown, with a tinge of purple-gray or smoky-brown ; head, neck, bill, and feet, black ; a patch of white on the cheek, behind the eye. Tail, of eighteen feathers.

B. leucopareia.—The White-cheeked Goose.

The White-cheeked Goose is smaller than the Canada Goose, and much darker in color. It is distinguished by a white cheek. Accidental in Canada. Habitat, British Columbia.

B. brenta.—The Brant.

This bird closely resembles the Canada Goose in its habits. It is twenty-four inches long. Bill, feet, head, tail, and neck, black. On each side of the middle of the neck is a small white crescent, streaked with black ; the belly, gray, passing into white behind.

Sub-Family ANATINÆ.—*The River Ducks.*

Anas boschas.—The Mallard, or Green-head.

This well known duck breeds in Canada. Nests, in a meadow, or near a pond ; eggs, ten or twelve, of a yellowish-white. The Green-head is the original of our domestic duck.

A. obscura.—The Black Duck, or Dusky Duck.

The Black Duck is the most abundant of all our ducks. Breeds in Canada. Nests, near a pond or stream ; eggs, six, white. General color, bluish-brown, tinged with black.

Dafila acuta.—The Pintail Duck.

This beautiful duck is a well known visitor in Canada. Head and neck, pale brown ; sides of the breast and part of the back, white, tinged with pale buff ; tail, pointed, the two middle feathers five inches longer than the others, and black ; legs, pale lead color. Breeds in the far north.

Nettion carolinensis.—The Green-winged Teal.

This pretty fowl is very abundant in Canada in the spring and fall. It frequently breeds here. Nests, on the ground, in close proximity to a pond or stream ; eggs, seven or eight in number, of a dusky-white color. This Teal is about fifteen inches in length ; the head is dusky ; the top of the head, cheeks, and neck are chestnut-red ; the throat is black ; a broad green band extends from the eye to the nape ; the lower part of the neck, back, and sides, are alternately striped with lines of white and black ; the breast is reddish, and spotted ; the belly, a yellowish-white.

Querquedala discors.—The Blue-winged Teal.

The Blue-winged Teal is a regular spring and fall visitor. This species is smaller than the preceding ; the bill is long, and of a dark dusky slate color ; the front and upper part of the head are black ; from the eye to the chin is a large crescent of white, the rest of the head and half the neck are of a dark slate, richly glossed with green and violet ; remainder of the neck and breast is black or dusky ; belly, pale brown, barred with dusky, in narrow lines ; back, deep brownish-black, each feather waived with large semi-ovals of brownish-white ; lesser wing coverts, a bright light blue. Habits similar to those of the Green-winged Teal.

Q. cyanoptera.—The Red-breasted Teal.

This pretty fowl occasionally visits our waters in company with the other Teals.

Spatula clypeata.—The Shoveller, or Spoonbill.

The Spoonbill breeds in the north-west. Visits Canada in the spring and autumn. Head and neck, green ; forepart, and sides of the breast, white ; rest of under parts, purplish-chestnut.

Chaulelasmus streperus.—The Gadwall, or
Gray Duck.

This species breeds in the far north. Visits Canada during the spring and fall migrations.

Head and neck, brownish-white; forepart of breast and back, blackish; underneath, plumbeous-gray.

Mareca americana.—Baldpate, or American Widgeon.

This beautiful fowl breeds in Manitoba. Visits Canada in company with Teals and Canvassback Ducks. Head and Neck, gray, spotted with · black; a broad green patch around and behind the eye; top of the head, nearly white.

SUMMER DUCK.

Aix sponsa.—The Summer Duck, or Wood Duck.

This bird is, without exception, the most beautiful of all our ducks. It builds its nest in a hollow tree, or on a limb that hangs over water ; eggs, twelve or thirteen, of a yellowish-white color. The Wood Duck is easily domesticated, and becomes quite tame, breeding, and soon acquiring all the habits of the common duck. Head and crest, greenish-purple, with white lines ; throat, white ; breast, reddish-brown, marked with white ; wings and back, green, with purple reflections ; sides, ashy-gray ; abdomen, white ; tail, purplish-green above, brown beneath ; the whole plumage beautifully variegated with purple, green, chestnut, white, and ashy.

Sub-Family FULIGULIN.E.—*The Sea Ducks.*

Fulix collaris.—The Ring-necked Duck.

This duck is distinguished by a chestnut collar around the middle of the neck. Color, above, black ; beneath, white. Frequents the Lower St. Lawrence in the fall.

F. marila.—The Scaup Duck, or Blue Bill.

The Scaup Duck breeds in the north-west. Visits Canada during the spring and autumn migrations, in small flocks. Head, neck, shoulders, back, and tail, black ; under parts, white ; bill, blue ; legs plumbeous ; iris, yellow.

F. affinis.—The Little Black-head Duck.

This pretty and well known bird sometimes breeds in Canada. It is often called "Blue-bill Coot" by our sportsmen. Head, neck, shoulders, lower part of back and tail, black ; belly, sides, and inner wing surfaces, pure white ; wings, blackish, with purple reflections.

Aythya americana.—The Red-head Duck.

This fine duck is generally very abundant in Canada. It breeds here. Head and neck, for more than half its length, brownish-red ; rest of neck and body anterior to the shoulders, and lower part of the back, black ; beneath, white.

A. vallisneria.—The Canvass-back Duck.

This much esteemed Duck is becoming quite rare in Ontario, where it was, a few years since, abundant. This duck is twenty-three or twenty-four inches long ; beak, large and black ; the head and part of the neck, of a rich, glossy reddish chestnut, ending in a broad span of black that covers the upper part of the breast ; back, scapulas, lower part of the breast, and belly, white ; tail, short and pointed ; legs and feet, pale ash. Breeds in northern Canada.

Bucephala islandica.—Barrow's Duck.

This duck breeds in the arctic regions. Visits Canada late in the fall. Head and neck, violet-blue ; a large white patch anterior to the eye ; lower neck and under parts, white ; a narrow white patch on the middle wing coverts ; rest of upper parts, black.

B. americana.—The Golden-eye, or Whistle Wing.

This duck breeds in Canada. Nests, in a tall dead tree, or in the top of a stub ; eggs, six or eight, of a greenish-blue color. Head and upper part of neck, green ; back and tail, black ; under parts, white.

B. albeola.—The Buffle-head, or Dipper.

This is a common and well known bird. It breeds in Canada. Nests, in the holes of dead trees ; eggs, six, of a yellowish-blue color. Color, above, black ; beneath, white ; in front of the eye and on the sides of the collar behind, rich green ; a patch of white on each side of the head.

Histrionicus torquatus.—The Harlequin Duck.

The Harlequin Duck breeds in the far north. Visits Canada in the fall. Head and neck, dark blue ; sides and upper parts, light blue, becoming darker near the tail ; under parts generally white.

14

Harelda glacialis.—The Long-tailed Duck, or Old Wife.

This duck is a frequent visitor during the spring and fall migrations. Breeds in the northern part of this continent. Head, neck, and breast, blackish-brown; sides of the head and body, bluish-gray; under parts, white.

Melanetta velvetina.—The Velvet Duck, or White-winged Coot.

The Velvet Duck is a regular fall visitor, usually arriving in October. General color, black; a white patch around and behind the eye, and a large white speculum on the wing.

Pelionetta perspicillata.—The Surf Duck.

The Surf Duck breeds in the northern part of Canada. Color, black, with a greenish lustre; a white patch on the top of the head.

Oidemia americana.—The Black Scoter.

The Black Scoter is an irregular visitor in Canada. General color, black.

Somateria mollissima.—The Eider Duck.

This well known duck breeds in abundance in Labrador and in northern Canada. During the fall and early winter it is occasionally shot near Toronto. Color, above, white; beneath, black; forehead and sides of the head, black.

S. spectabilis.—The King Duck, or King Eider.

This is a more northern species than the preceding. It is seldom seen in Ontario. Specimens are occasionally obtained in the Gulf of St. Lawrence. Length, twenty-one and a-half inches. Body and wings, black; throat, white; top of head, bluish-ash; sides of the head, green.

Sub-Family ERISMATURINÆ.

Erismatura rubida.—The Ruddy Duck, or Dipper.

The Ruddy Duck is a spring and fall visitor. Length, sixteen inches; color, chestnut-red above; grayish-white below; top of head, black. Visits Canada during the fall migrations.

E. dominica.—The Black-masked Duck.

This species is an accidental visitor in Canada. Its habitat is Labrador, the Lower St. Lawrence, and Lake Champlain.

Sub-Family MERGINÆ.—*The Sheldrakes.*

Mergus serrator.—The Red-breasted Merganser.

The Red-breasted Merganser breeds in Canada. The head and neck is dark green ; under parts, yellowish-white. Head with a conspicuous crest. Nests, in a marsh, or on an island ; eggs, ten, light drab.

M. americanus.—The Goosander, or Fish Duck.

This beautiful fowl frequently breeds in Ontario. It builds its nest on the top of a tall stump, or on the branch of a dead tree ; eggs, eight in number, of a pale creamy white. Head and neck, green ; back, black ; under parts, salmon color ; wings, white, crossed by a band of black.

HOODED MERGANSER.

Lophodytes cucullatus.—The Hooded Merganser.

This elegant bird is not so common as the other Mergansers. It breeds in Canada. Nests, in the top of a stub or in a tall pine ; eggs, twelve or fourteen in number, of a clear white color. This species is eighteen inches long ; the head, neck, and tail, black ; the under parts and centre of the crest, white.

SUB-ORDER GAVIÆ.

FAMILY PELICANIDÆ. *THE PELICANS.*

Pelicanus fuscus.—The Brown Pelican.

The Brown Pelican is fifty-six inches long ; bill, thirteen and a-half inches ; color, dark. Several specimens of this fine bird have been shot in Ontario within the last two years. They are accidental visitors.

P. erythrorhynchus.—The Rough-billed Pelican.

This magnificent bird is seventy inches in length ; the prevailing color, white. It is an occasional visitor in Ontario.

FAMILY SULIDÆ. *THE GANNETS.*

Sula bassana.—The Common Gannet.

This species breeds on the coast of Labrador and in the Gulf of St. Lawrence. Visits Ontario in the fall, in flocks of twenty or thirty. Length, thirty eight inches ; general color, white. Feeds upon fish, which it obtains by plunging from a height, often remaining under water for several minutes. The nest of the gannet is made of sea-weed and grasses, placed on the rocks near the sea coast. It lays but one egg, of a pale green color.

Family GRACULIDÆ. *THE CORMORANTS.*

Graculus carbo.—The Common Cormorant.

This species breeds in Canada. They are quite common in the interior of the country. Nests, in the crevices of rocks ; eggs, three of a bluish-green color. Among the whole of the web-footed birds which prey on fish, there are none so voracious as Cormorants. They are most excellent divers, and pursue their prey with astonishing facility beneath the surface of the water, but upon land they are extremely awkward in their movements, owing to their legs being placed so far backwards : they, however, fly with rapidity ; and the tail being rather long, and furnished with strong feathers, it helps to support the body while walking. As soon as winter approaches, they are seen dispersed along the sea shores, entering the mouths of fresh-water rivers, and threatening destruction to all the finny tribe. The Common Cormorant is thirty-seven inches in length; the color, bluish-black, gular sac, yellow, with a broad white band at the base.

DOUBLE-CRESTED CORMORANT.

Graculus dilophus.—The Double-crested Cormorant.

This species is not so well known as the preceding. Its habits are similar to the Common Cormorant. Breeds in Labrador. The head, neck, lower part of the back, and entire under surface, is greenish-black; upper mandible, dark brown; lower, yellow; iris, green; legs and feet, black; gular sac, orange; behind each eye is a tuft of loose feathers, which form the crest.

FAMILY LARIDÆ. *THE GULLS.*

Sub-Family LESTRIDINÆ.—*The Skua Gulls.*

Stercorarius parasiticus.—The Arctic Skua.

The Arctic Skua breeds in the northern part of this continent. During the winter it frequents the sea coast of Canada. Length, twenty-two inches; color, above, brownish-black; beneath, white.

S. pomarinus.—The Pomarine Skua.

This species breeds in the far north. It is much more common than the preceding. Color, dark brown, tinged with black, above; beneath, white. Length, twenty inches. A regular visitor to the sea coast of Nova Scotia and Newfoundland.

Sub-Family LARINÆ.—*The Gulls.*

Larus marinus.—The Great Black-backed Gull.

This fine bird is twenty-six inches in length; the bill is pale yellow, thick and strong; upper parts of the back and wing, black; all the other parts of its plumage, white; legs, pale flesh color. Breeds in Labrador. Is a fall, and, sometimes, winter visitor in Canada.

Larus Sabinii.—The Fork-tailed Gull.

This gull frequents the coast of New Brunswick and Nova Scotia. Head and upper part of neck, blackish-gray ; lower neck, lower parts, and tail, white ; back and wings, bluish-gray ; tail, long and forked.

L. Rossii.—Ross's Gull.

The habitat of this pretty gull is the arctic regions. During the fall and winter a few specimens are occasionally seen in the Gulf of St. Lawrence, and on the coast of Nova Scotia and Newfoundland. Back and wings, grayish-blue ; neck, lower parts, and tail, white ; bill, black ; feet, red. Discovered by Sir James Clark Ross, the navigator.

L. Franklinii.—Franklin's Gull.

This gull is a rare visitor in Canada. Its habitat is the arctic regions. Bill and feet, vermillion ; neck, rump, tail, and under plumage, white ; black hood on nape; upper parts, bluish-gray ; quills, terminated with white.

L. argentatus.—The Herring Gull, or Silvery Gull.

The Silvery Gull is a regular visitor in Canada. It is twenty-four inches long ; bill, yellow ; head, neck, and tail, white ; the back and wing coverts, bluish-ash ; legs, pale flesh color. Breeds in the north.

15

L. canus.—The Common Gull.

The Common Gull is the most numerous of the family. It is seventeen inches long; bill, yellow; head, neck, tail, and whole under side of the body, white; the back and coverts of the wings are gray.

L. glaucus.—The Glaucous Gull.

This gull breeds in the arctic regions. An accidental visitor in Canada.

L. leucopterus.—The White-winged Gull.

This species breeds in the far north. A rare visitor.

L. delawarensis.—The Ring-billed Gull.

This gull is a rare visitor in Canada.

L. eburneus.—The Ivory Gull.

This beautiful gull is very common in the arctic regions, and occasionally visits Canada in the fall and winter.

Creagrus furcatus.—The Swallow-tailed Gull.

This pretty gull is an accidental visitor in Canada. Its habitat is the Pacific coast.

Chroicocephalus atricilla.—The Laughing Gull.

This little gull is a summer resident of Canada. The head and upper part of the neck is blackish-gray; lower part of neck and entire under plumage, pure white; back and wings, grayish-lead color. Breeds in Canada. Nests, in marshes; eggs, three, of an olive-drab color.

C. philadelphia.—Bonaparte's Gull.

This well known gull is a summer resident of Canada. Back and wings, clear bluish-gray; under plumage, rump and tail, white; length, fourteen inches.

Rissa tridactyla.—The Kittiwake Gull.

The Kittiwake Gull occasionally visits Lake Ontario during the fall. The head, neck, and under plumage is pure white; back and wings, light bluish-gray; bill, greenish-yellow; legs, brownish-black.

Sub-Family STERINÆ.—*The Terns.*

Sterna aranea.—The Marsh Tern.

This pretty tern is a regular visitor. Head, black; back and wings, light bluish-gray; under plumage, pure white; bill, legs, and feet, black.

S. caspia.—The Caspian Tern.

The Caspian Tern is a fall and winter visitor. Head, black, glossed with green; back and wings, light bluish-ash ; under plumage, pure white; bill, and inside of mouth, bright red ; legs and feet, black.; tail, forked. Breeds in the northern regions.

S. *Wilsonii.*—Wilson's Tern.

This is the most common species in Canada. Head, deep black, tinged with brown ; back and wings, light grayish-blue ; breast and abdomen, clear pearl gray. Breeds on the sea coast of New Brunswick.

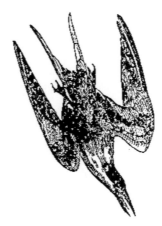

ARCTIC TERN.

S. *arctica.*—The Arctic Tern.

The Arctic Tern is a fall and winter visitor in Ontario. Breeds on the sea coast of Nova Scotia. Head and neck, black ; back and wings, light grayish-blue ; under parts, bluish-gray, of a lighter shade than the back ; legs and feet, crimson ; bill, deep carmine..

S. frenata.—The Least Tern.

The Least Tern is an irregular visitor. Breeds on the sea coast. Length, nine inches ; color, bluish-gray above ; underneath, white ; bill, orange ; legs and feet, orange-red.

S. fuliginosa.—The Sooty Tern.

This tern is a regular summer visitor. Head, neck, and abdomen, black ; back and wings, plumbeous-gray.

S. paridisea.—The Roseate Tern.

The Roseate Tern is an irregular summer visitor in Canada.

Rhynchops nigra.—Black Skimmer, or Sheerwater.

This fowl occasionally visits Lake Ontario in the spring, retiring south to breed in June. Color : head, neck, and wings, black ; throat, breast, and abdomen, white ; legs, scarlet ; length of the upper mandible, three inches and a-half ; of the lower, four inches and a-half. The peculiar formation of its bill, the lower mandible being one inch longer than the upper, enables it easily to obtain its food while skimming over the surface of the water.

Sub-Family COLYMBINÆ.—*The Loons.*

GREAT NORTHERN DIVER.

Colymbus torquatus.—The Great Northern Diver,
or Loon.

The Great Northern Diver is a resident of
Canada.   Nests, on an island, or in a meadow or
marsh, near the borders of the interior lakes ;
eggs, two or three in number, of a reddish brown
color, with an olive tint.   This bird is twenty-
eight inches in length.   Head and neck, bluish-
green ; upper plumage and wing coverts, deep
glossy black, marked with white spots.

C. septentrionalis.—The Red-throated Diver.

This species is not so common as the Great
Northern Diver, usually arriving here in October

from the coast of Labrador, where it breeds. Color, above, brownish-black, tinged with green ; underneath, white ; bill, bluish-black; iris, bright red ; feet, brownish-black.

Sub-Family PODICIPINÆ.—*The Grebes.*

Podiceps griseigena.—The Red-necked Grebe.

The Red-necked Grebe breeds in the far north ; visits Canada in the fall. Upper parts, blackish-brown ; lower parts, pure white ; bill, black ; feet, greenish-black. Length, eighteen inches.

P. cristatus.—The Crested Grebe.

This Grebe is a common summer resident of Canada. It is chiefly valued for the plumage of its breast, the flesh being rank and nauseous. Color, above, umber-brown ; beneath, pure white ; long tufts on each side of the head, of umber-brown color. Nests, in a swamp or marsh ; eggs, four in number, white.

P. cornutus.—The Horned Grebe.

The Horned Grebe breeds in northern Canada. Visits Ontario in the fall. Color, above, brownish-black ; breast, bright chestnut ; abdomen, white ; bill, bluish-black ; feet, dark gray.

Podilymbus podiceps.—The Pied-billed Grebe.

This species is a common summer resident of Canada. Upper parts, dark brown ; breast and abdomen, grayish-white, mottled with dusky spots.

Family PBOCELLARIDÆ. *THE PETRELS.*

Thalassidroma Leaehii.—Leach's Petrel.

Leach's Petrel breeds on the sea coast of New Brunswick and Nova Scotia. The general color of this bird is sooty-brown ; bill and feet, black. Length, eight inches. Nests, in the crevices of rocks. Lays one pure white egg.

STORMY PETREL.

T. Wilsonii.—Wilson's Stormy Petrel.

This Petrel is seven inches in length. Color, deep sooty-black ; tail, green ; wings reaching a little beyond its tip; tarsus, one and a-half inches in length. Breeds on the small islands off the coast of Nova Scotia. Its habits and general color are similar to those of Leach's Petrel. This is the bird so much dreaded by sailors as the harbinger of a storm, and to which they have given the name of " Mother Carey's Chicken." It is met with on every part of the ocean, diving or skimming over the surface of the rolling waves of the most tempestuous sea. Captain Sir James Clark Ross, in his "Voyage to the Antarctic Regions," observes that, when in lat. 47° 17' S., long. 58° 50' E., " we were accompanied on our course by petrels of two or three different kinds. These birds added a degree of cheerfulness to our solitary wanderings, which contrasted strongly with the dreary and unvarying stillness of the tropical region, where not a sea-bird is to be seen, except only in the vicinity of its few scattered islets, which is the more remarkable where the ocean abounds so plentifully with creatures fit for their food."

Sub-Family PUFFINUS.

Puffinus cinereus.—Wandering Shearwater.

This bird frequents the sea coast of the maritime provinces. Upper parts, deep brown; lower parts, grayish-white; bill, yellowish-green; feet, light greenish-gray; length, twenty inches.

16

Puffinus major.—The Greater Shearwater.

The Greater Shearwater frequents the extreme eastern coast of Canada. Length, twenty inches; brownish-ash, above; grayish-white, below; bill, compressed near the end; a straight spur in place of a hind toe.

Puffinus anglorum.—Mank's Shearwater.

Habitat, the coast of New Brunswick, Nova Scotia, and Newfoundland. Upper parts, brownish-black; lower, white; bill, greenish-black. Length, fourteen inches. Breeds in burrows; lays one white egg.

Puffinus obscurus.—Dusky Shearwater.

This bird frequents the coast of New Brunswick and the Gulf of St. Lawrence. Upper parts, sooty-black; lower, white; bill, light blue. Length, eleven inches.

FAMILY ALCIDÆ.

Sub-Family ALCINÆ.—*The Auks.*

Alca impennis.—The Great Auk.

The Greak Auk is becoming very rare: a few specimens are occasionally seen on the coast of Newfoundland and Nova Scotia. Color: head, neck, and upper parts, black ; lower parts, white. Nests, on the sand ; eggs, two, reddish-brown.

Alca torda.—The Razor-billed Auk.

The Razor-billed Auk is seventeen inches in length. The general form of this bird is short and heavy ; bill, long ; upper parts, brownish-black ; under parts, white. Frequents the sea coast of Nova Scotia and Newfoundland. Breeds in the arctic region. They build no nests, but lay their eggs upon the bare edges of lofty rocks overhanging the sea. Large numbers of these birds are killed on the coast for the sake of their breast feathers.

Mormon glacialis.—Large-billed Puffin.

This bird frequents the Bay of Fundy and the sea coast of New Brunswick. Bill and feet, orange-yellow ; sides of the head and lower parts, white ; a dark grayish color extends to the lower mandible.

ARCTIC PUFFIN.

Mormon arctica.—The Arctic Puffin.

This exceedingly quaint looking bird is twelve inches in length. It has a very large bill, which has the appearance of a sheath slipped over both mandibles ; it is curved towards the point, compressed vertically, and transversely furrowed on the sides ; the chin and cheeks are white, bordered with gray, the latter much puffed up with feathers, which makes the head look large and round. The crown of the head and upper part of the plumage are black, and a collar of the same color encircles the neck; the under parts are white, and the legs are orange. The female deposits her single whitish-colored egg in a hole dug out and formed in the ground by her mate and herself, or in one ready-made by the rabbits, which they easily dislodge. Puffins are met with on almost all the rocky cliffs on the coasts of Nova Scotia and Newfoundland, and on many of the surrounding islands. They are gregarious and migratory.

Sub-Family URINÆ.—*The Guillemots.*

BLACK GUILLEMOT.

Uria grylle.—The Black Guillemot.

The Black Guillemot is thirteen inches in length. Color, black; a white patch on each wing. This bird is a resident of eastern Canada throughout the year. It breeds on the rocky islands off the coast of New Brunswick; eggs, three in number, pure white.

Uria lomvia.—The Foolish Guillemot.

This species is seventeen inches in length. The head, neck, back, wings, and tail, are of a slate color; the breast and abdomen, white. This bird is very common on the coast of New Brunswick, where they occasionally breed.

Uria Brunswickii.—Large-billed Guillemot.

This Guillemot frequents the coast of New Brunswick. Color, above, grayish-black; abdomen and edges of the wings, white; bill, black; feet, dusky; eggs, three, bluish-green, laid in the sand.

Uria ringvia.—The Murre.

The Murre is the same size as the preceding; upper parts, dark brown, with a tinge of ash; under parts, white. Frequents the coast of Nova Scotia and New Brunswick.

Mergulus alle.—The Arctic Sea Dove.

This species is only eight inches in length. Color, brownish black, above; white, beneath. This bird is a winter visitor to the sea coast of Canada.

BIRDS

OF

MANITOBA AND BRITISH COLUMBIA.

As the Provinces of British Columbia and Manitoba now form part of the Dominion of Canada, I append a classified catalogue of those birds whose migrations extend from South America, California, and the Great Plains, to British Columbia and Manitoba, not including those already mentioned in the body of this work, whose migrations extend eastward from the above Provinces.

RAPTORES, OR BIRDS OF PREY.

Falco vulgaris—Common Buzzard.
Stix cunicularia—Burrowing Owl.
    "   *passerinoides*—Columbia Day Owl.

INSESSORES, OR PERCHERS.

Hirundo thallasima—Violet-green Swallow.
Musicicapæ verticalis—Arkansas Flycatcher.
    "   *nigricans*—Rocky Mountain Flycatcher.
    "   *Phœbe*—Short-legged Pewit.

INSESSORES—*Continued.*

Musicicapæ Trailli—Traill's Flycatcher.
    "   *pusilla*—Least Pewee.
Ptilogonys Townsendi—Townsend's Ptilogonys.
Turdus nævius—Varied Thrush.
    "   *nanus*—Dwarf Thrush.
    "   *montanus*—Mountain Mocking Bird.
Cinclus americanus—American Dipper.
Sylviæ Audubonii—Audubon's Warbler.
    "   *Townsendii*—Townsend's Warbler.
    "   *occidentalis*—Hermit Warbler.
Troglodytes obsoletus—Rock Wren.
    "   *Parkmanii*—Parkman's Wren
Sialia occidentalis—Western Blue Bird.
    "   *arctica*—Arctic Blue Bird.
Parus minimus—Chestnut-crowned Tit.
    "   *Hudsonicus*—Hudson's Bay Tit.
Fringilla Townsendii—Townsend's Finch.
    "   *cinera*—Brown Finch.
    "   *Mortonii*—Morton's Finch.
    "   *Oregonii*—Oregon Snow Bird.
    "   *frontalis*—Crimson-fronted Finch.
    "   *bephrocotis*—Gray-crowned Finch.
Enteriza pallida—Clay-colored Bunting.
    "   *lapponica*—Lapland Lark Bunting.
    "   *ornata*—Chestnut-colored Lark Bunting.
Spiza amœna—Lazuli Painted Bunting.
Carduelis psalteri—Arkansas Goldfinch.
Pipilo arcticus—Arctic Ground Finch.

INSESSORES—*Continued.*

Corydalina tricolor—Prairie Lark Finch.

Coccothraustes melanocephalus—Black-headed Grosbeak.

" *vespertina*—Evening Grosbeak.

" *cærulea*—Blue Grosbeak.

Icterus Bullockii—Bullock's Hangnest.

" *xanthrocephalus*—Saffron-headed Blackbird.

Corvus Nuttallii—Yellow-billed Magpie.

" *Bullockii*—Columbian Magpie.

Garrulus Stelleri.—Steller's Jay.

" *ultramarinus.*—Ultramarine Jay.

Trochilus Anna—Anna Humming Bird.

" *rufus*—Rufous-ruffed Humming Bird.

SCANSORES, or CLIMBERS.

Picus lineatus—Lineated Woodpecker.

" *canadensis*—Canadian Woodpecker.

" *Harrissii*—Harris's Woodpecker.

" *Gardnerii*—Gardner's Woodpecker.

" *arcticus*—Arctic Three-toed Woodpecker.

" *mexicans*—Red-shafted Woodpecker.

RASORES, or SCRATCHERS.

Tetrao leucurus—White-tailed Ptarmigan.

" *rupestris*—Rock Ptarmigan.

" *mutus*—American Ptarmigan.

" *Phasianellus*—Sharp-tailed Grouse.

17

Tetrao urophasianus—Cock of the Plains.
" *obscurus*—Dusky Grouse.
Ortyx plumifera—Plumed Partridge.
Columba fasciata—Band-tailed Pigeon.

GRALLATORES, or WADERS.

Scollopax Drummondii—Drummond's Snipe.
Hæmatopus Townsendii—Townsend's Oyster-
catcher.
Aphriza Townsendii—Townsend's Surf Bird.
Charadrius montanus—Rocky Mountain Plover.

NATTATORES, or SWIMMERS.

Uria Townsendii—Slender-billed Guillemot.
" *occidentalis*—Horn-billed Guillemot.
" *antiqua*—Black-throated Guillemot.
Phaleris nodirostris—Knob-billed Phaleris.
" *cristaletta*—Curled-crested Phaleris.
Procellaria tenuirstris—Slender-billed Fulmar.
" *pacifica*—Pacific Fulmar.
" *gigantica*—Gigantic Fulmar.
Diomeda fusca—Dusky Albatross.
" *chlorrorhynchus*—Yellow-nosed Albatross.
Phalacrocorax resplendens—Violet-green Cormorant.
" *Townsendii*—Townsend's Cormorant.
Fuligula despar—Western Duck.
Anser Hutchinsii—Hutchin's Goose.

SYNOPSIS

OF

BIRDS OF CANADA.

SCIENTIFIC NAMES.

ORDER I.—RAPTORES.

Falco anatum.
" columbarius.
Tinnunculus sparverius.
Astur atricapillus.
Accipiter Cooperii.
" fuscus.
Buteo borealis.
" lineatus.
" pennsylvanicus.
Archibuteo lagopus.
" sancti johannis.
Circus hudsonius.
Haliætus leucocephalus.

Aquila canadensis.
Pandion carolinensis.
Bubo virginianis.
Scops asio.
Otus Wilsonianus.
Brachyotus Cassinii.
Syrnium nebulosum.
" cinereum.
Nyctale Richardsonii.
" acadica.
Nyctea nivea.
Surnia ulula.

ORDER II.—SCANSORES.

Coccygus americanus.
" erythropthalmus.
Picus villosus.
" pubescens.
Picoides arcticus.
" hursutus.

Sphyrapicus varius.
Hylatomus pileatus.
Melanerpes erythroce-
  phalus.
Colaptes auratus.
Centurces carolinensis.

ORDER III.—INSESSORES.

Trochilus colubris.
Chetura pelasgia.
Hirundo americana.
    " lunifrons.
    " riparia.
    " bicolor.
Progne purpurea.
Caprimulgus vociferus.
    " carolinensis.
Chordeiles popetue.
Ceryle alcyon.
Tyrannus carolinensis.
Myiarchus crinitus.
Sayornis fuscus.
Contopus virens.
Empidonax minimus.
Turdus mustelinus.
    " pallassii.
    " fuscescens.
    " Swainsonii.
    " migratorius.
Harporhynchus rufous.
Galeoscoptes carolinen-
    sis.
Sialia sialis.
Regulus calendula.
Regulus satrapa.
Regulus Cuvieri.
Parus atricapillus.
Sitta carolinensis.
    " canadensis.
Certhia americana.

Cistothorus palustris.
Troglodytes hyemalis.
    " ædon.
Mniotilta varia.
Parula americana.
Geothlypis trichas.
    " philadelphiæ.
    " Macgillvrai.
Sylvia trichas.
Dendroica virens.
    " palmarum.
    " tigrina.
    " canadensis.
    " coronata.
    " Blackburniæ.
    " castanea.
    " pinus.
    " pennsyl-
        vanica.
    " striata.
    " æstiva.
    " maculosa.
Myiodioctes canadensis.
    " mitratis.
    " minutus.
    " pusillus.
Helmitherus vermivo-
    rus.
Helminthopaga pinus.
    " chrysoptera.
    " ruficapilla.

ORDER III.—INSESSORES.—*Continued.*

Helminthopaga pere-
grina.
Icteria viridis.
Setophaga ruticilla.
Seiurus aurocapillus.
" noveboracensis.
Pyranga rubra.
Ampelis cedrorum.
Collyrio borealis.
" excubitorides.
Vireo olivaceous
" gilvus.
" noveboracensis.
" flavifrons.
" solitarius.
Eremophila cornuta.
Pinicola canadensis.
Carpodacus purpureus.
Chrysomitris tristis.
" pinus.
Curvirostra americana.
" leucoptera.
Ægiothus linaria.
Plectrophanes nivalis.
" Lapponicus.
Passerculus savanna.
Poocætes gramineus.
Coturniculus passerinus.
Zonotrichia leucophrys.

Zonotrichia albicollis.
Junco hyemalis.
Spizella monticola.
" pusilla.
" socialis.
Melospiza melodia.
" palustris.
Passerella iliaca.
Emberiza americana.
Guiraca Ludoviciana.
" cœrula.
Coccothraustes vesper-
tina.
" cardinalis.
Cyanospiza cyanea.
Pipilo erythropthalmus.
Dolichonyx oryzivorus.
Molothrus pecoris.
Agelaius phœniceus.
Sturnella magna.
Icterus spurius.
" baltimore.
Scolecophagus ferrugi-
neus.
Quiscalus versicolor.
Corvus americanus.
" corax.
Cyanurus cristatus.
Perisoreus canadensis.

ORDER IV.—RASORES.

Ectopistes migratoria.
Zenaidura carolinensis.
Tetrao canadensis.
Bonasa umbellus.

Tetrao phasianellus.
Ortyx virginianus.
Meleagris gallopavo.

ORDER V.—GRALLATORES.

Ardea herodias.
Ardetta exilis.
Botaurus lentignosus.
Butorides virescens.
Nyctiardea Gardenii.
Grus canadensis.
" americana.
Ibis falcinellus.
Charadrius virginicus.
Ægialitis vociferus.
" Wilsonius.
" semi-palmatus.
" melodus.
" montanus.
Squatarola helvetica.
Hæmatopus palliatus.
" niger.
Strepsilas interpres.
" melanocephala.
Recurvirostra ameri-
cana.
Phalaropus hyper-
boreus.
" Wilsonii.
" fulicarius.
Philohela minor.

Gallinago Wilsonii.
Macrorhamphus griseus.
" scolopaceus.
Tringa canutus.
" Cooperii.
" maritima.
" subarquata.
" alpina.
" maculata.
" Wilsonii.
" Bonapartii.
Calidris arenaria.
Ereunetes petrificatus.
Micropalma himan-
topus.
Symphemia semi-pal-
mata.
Gambetta melanoleuca.
" flavipes.
Rhyacophilus solitarius.
Tringoides macularius.
Actiturus Bartramius.
Tringites rufescens.
Limosa fedoa.
" hudsonica.

ORDER V.—GRALLATORES.—*Continued.*

Numenius longirostris.
"   borealis.
"   hudsonicus.
Rallus elegans.
"   crepitans.
"   virginianus.

Porzana carolina.
"   noveboracensis.
"   jamaicensis.
Crex pratensis.
Fulica americana.
Gallinule martinica.

ORDER VI.—NATATORES.

Cygnus americanus.
"   buccinator.
Anser hyperboreus.
"   Gambelli.
"   frontalis.
Bernicla canadensis.
"   leucopareia.
"   brenta.
Anas boschas.
"   obscura.
Dafila acuta.
Nettion carolinensis.
Querquedula discors.
"   cyanoptera.
Spatula clypeata.
Chaulelasmus streperus.
Mareca americana.
Aix sponsa.
Fulix marila.
"   affinis.
"   collaris.
Aythya vallisneria.
"   americana.

Bucephala islandica.
Bucephala albeola.
Histrionicus torquatus.
Harelda glacialis.
Melanetta velvetina.
Pelionetta perspicillata.
Oidemia americana.
Somateria mollissima.
"   spectabalis.
Erismatura rubida.
"   dominica.
Mergus serrator.
"   americanus.
Lophodytes cucullatus.
Pelicanus fuscus.
"   erythrorhynchus.
Sula bassana.
Graculus carbo.
"   dilophus.
Stercorarus parasiticus.
"   pomarinis.
Larus marinus.
"   argentatus.
"   Rossii.

ORDER VI.—NATATORES.—*Continued.*

Larus Franklinii.
    "   Sabinii.
    "   canus.
    "   leucopterus.
    "   delawarensis.
    "   eberneus.
Creagrus furcatus.
Chroicocephalus a t r i -
          cilla.
    "   philadelphia.
Rissa tridactyla.
Sterna aranea.
    "   caspia.
    "   Wilsonii.
    "   arctica.
    "   frenata.
    "   fulignosa.
    "   paridisea.
Colymbus septentrio-
    nalis.

Colymbus torquatus,
Podiceps griseigena.
    "   cristatus.
    "   cornutus.
Podilymbus podiceps.
Thalassidroma Wilsonii.
    "   Leachii.
Puffinus major.
    "   cinereus.
    "   anglorum.
    "   obscurus.
Alca impennis.
    "   torda.
Mergulus alle.
Mormon arctica.
    "   glacialis.
Uria grylle.
    "   lomvia.
    "   ringvia.
    "   Brunswickii.

SYNOPSIS

OF

BIRDS OF CANADA.

COMMON NAMES.

ORDER I.—BIRDS OF PREY.

Peregrine. Falcon, or Duck Hawk.
Sparrow Hawk.
Pigeon Hawk.
Goshawk.
Cooper's Hawk.
Sharp-shinned Hawk.
Red-tailed Hawk.
Red-shouldered Hawk.
Broad-winged Hawk.
Rough-legged Hawk.
Black Hawk.
Marsh Hawk.
White-headed Eagle.

Golden Eagle.
Fish Hawk.
Great Horned Owl.
Mottled Owl, or Screech Owl.
Long-eared Owl.
Short-eared Owl.
Barred Owl.
Cinereous Owl.
Sparrow Owl.
Saw-whet Owl.
Snowy Owl.
Hawk Owl.

ORDER II.—CLIMBERS.

Yellow-billed Cuckoo.
Black-billed Cuckoo.
Hairy Woodpecker.
Downy Woodpecker.
Black-backed Three-toed Woodpecker.
Banded Three-toed Woodpecker.
Pileated Woodpecker.

Yellow-bellied Woodpecker.
Red-headed Woodpecker.
Golden-winged Woodpecker.
Red-bellied Woodpecker.

18

ORDER III.—PERCHERS.

Ruby - throated Humming Bird.
Chimney Swallow.
Barn Swallow.
Cliff Swallow.
White-breasted Swallow.
Bank Swallow.
Purple Martin.
Whip-poor-will.
Chuck-Will's Widow.
Night Hawk.
Belted Kingfisher.
King Bird.
Great - crested Flycatcher.
Phebe Bird.
Wood Pewee.
Least Flycatcher.
Wood Thrush.
Hermit Thrush.
Tawny Thrush.
Olive-backed Thrush.
Robin.
Brown Thrasher.
Cat Bird.
Blue Bird.
Ruby-crowned Wren.
Golden-crested Wren.
Cuvier's Golden-crested Wren.
Black-cap Titmouse.
White-bellied Nuthatch.
Red-bellied Nuthatch.
American Creeper.
Long - billed Marsh Wren.
Winter Wren.
House Wren.
Black and White Creeper.
Blue Yellow - backed Warbler.
Maryland Yellow-throat.
Mourning Warbler.
Gray-headed Warbler.
Macgillivray's Warbler.
Black - throated Green Warbler.
Yellow Red-poll Warbler.
Cape May Warbler.
Black - throated Blue Warbler.
Yellow-rump Warbler.
Blackburnian Warbler.
Bay-breasted Warbler.
Pine-creeping Warbler.
Chestnut-sided Warbler.
Black-poll Warbler.
Yellow Warbler.
Black and Yellow Warbler.
Canada Flycatcher.
Hooded Warbler.

ORDER III.—PERCHERS.—*Continued.*

Small - headed Fly-catcher.
Green Black-cap Fly-catcher.
Worm-eating Warbler.
Blue - winged Yellow Warbler.
Golden-winged Warb-ler.
Nashville Warbler.
Tennessee Warbler.
Yellow-breasted Chat.
Red Start.
Golden - crowned Thrush.
Water Thrush, or Wag-tail.
Scarlet Tanager.
Bohemian Chatterer.
Cedar Bird, or Cherry Bird.
Great Northern Shrike.
White-rumped Shrike.
Red-eyed Vireo.
Warbling Vireo.
White-eyed Vireo.
Solitary Vireo.
Yellow-throated Vireo.
Shore Lark.
Pine Grosbeak.
Purple Finch.
Yellow Bird.
Pine Finch.

Red Crossbill.
White-winged Crossbill.
Lesser Red-poll.
Snow Bunting.
Savannah Sparrow.
Bay-winged Bunting.
White - crowned Spar-row.
White - throated Spar-row.
Snow Bird.
Tree Sparrow.
Field Sparrow.
Chipping Sparrow.
Song Sparrow.
Swamp Sparrow.
Fox-colored Sparrow.
Rose - breasted Gros-beak.
Indigo Bird.
Ground Robin, or Che-wink.
Bobolink.
Cow Bird.
Red-winged Blackbird.
Meadow Lark.
Orchard Oriole.
Baltimore Oriole.
Rusty Grackle.
Purple Grackle.
Crow.
Blue Jay.
Canada Jay.

ORDER IV.—SCRATCHERS.

Wild Pigeon.
Carolina Dove.
Spruce Partridge.
Ruffled Grouse, or Partridge.

Virginia Partridge, or Quail.
Wild Turkey.

ORDER V.—WADERS.

Great Blue Heron.
Least Bittern.
Great Bittern.
Green Heron.
Night Heron.
Sandhill Crane.
White Crane.
Golden Plover.
Kill-deer Plover.
Mountain Plover.
Wilson's Plover.
Semi-palmated Plover.
Piping Plover.
Black-bellied Plover.
Oyster-catcher.
Backman's Oyster-catcher.
Turnstone.
Black Turnstone.
American Avoset.
Northern Phalarope.
Wilson's Phalarope.
Red Phalarope.
Woodcock.
Wilson's Snipe.

Gray Snipe.
Longbeak.
Gray - back, or Robin Snipe.
Cooper's Sandpiper.
Purple Sandpiper.
Curlew Sandpiper.
Red-backed Sandpiper.
Jack Snipe.
Least Sandpiper.
Bonaparte's Sandpiper.
Sanderling.
Semi - palmated Sandpiper.
Stilt Sandpiper.
Willet.
Tell-tale.
Yellow Legs.
Solitary Sandpiper.
Spotted Sandpiper.
Field Plover.
Buff - breasted Sandpiper.
Marbled Godwit.
Hudsonian Godwit.

ORDER V.—WADERS.—*Continued.*

Long-billed Curlew.
Short-billed Curlew.
Esquimaux Curlew.
Marsh Hen.
Clapper Rail.
Virginia Rail.

Carolina Rail.
Little Black Rail.
Yellow Rail.
Corn Crake.
Coot.
Purple Gallinule.

ORDER VI.—SWIMMERS.

American Swan.
Trumpeter Swan.
Snow Goose.
Canada Goose, or Wild Goose.
White-fronted Goose.
Brown-fronted Goose.
White-cheeked Goose.
Brant.
Green-head Duck.
Black Duck.
Pintail Duck.
Green-winged Teal.
Blue-winged Teal.
Red-breasted Teal.
Shoveller Duck.
Gadwall, or Gray Duck.
Baldpate, or American Widgeon.
Wood Duck.
Scaup Duck.
Little Black-head Duck.
Red-Head Duck.
Canvas-backed Duck.
Golden Eye, or Barrow's Duck.

Whistle Wing Duck.
Buffle-head, or Dipper.
Harlequin Duck.
Long-tailed Duck, or Old Wife.
Velvet Duck, or White-winged Coot.
Surf Duck.
Eider Duck.
King Duck, or King Eider.
Ruddy Duck.
Black-masked Duck.
Red-breasted Merganser.
Goosander, or Fish Duck.
Hooded Merganser.
Brown Pelican.
Rough-billed Pelican.
Common Gannet.
Common Cormorant.
Double-crested Cormorant.
Great Black-backed Gull.

ORDER VI.—SWIMMERS.—*Continued.*

Herring Gull.
Arctic Skua.
Pomarine Skua.
Glaucous-winged Gull.
Ross's Gull.
Franklin's Gull.
Fork-tailed Gull.
Common Gull.
Glaucous Gull.
White-winged Gull.
Ring-billed Gull.
Swallow-tailed Gull.
Ivory Gull.
Laughing Gull.
Bonaparte's Gull.
Kittiwake Gull.
Marsh Tern.
Caspian Tern.
Wilson's Tern.
Arctic Tern.
Least Tern.
Sooty Tern.
Roseate Tern.

Great Northern Diver.
Red-throated Diver.
Red-necked Grebe.
Crested Grebe.
Horned Grebe.
Pied-billed Grebe.
Leach's Petrel.
Wilson's Petrel.
Greater Shearwater, or
 Petrel.
Wandering Shearwater.
Mank's Shearwater.
Dusky Shearwater.
Great Auk.
Razor-billed Auk.
Little Auk.
Arctic Puffin.
Large-billed Guillemot.
Large-billed Puffin.
Black Guillemot.
Foolish Guillemot.
Murre.
Arctic Sea Dove.

INDEX.

19

Printed in Great Britain
by Amazon

69102084R00102